Teaching Children:
Karate and More

Library of Congress Control Number: 2015941259
ISBN: Softcover   978-0-9792736-0-5

Teaching Children:
Karate and More

Michelle Darbro

Dedication and Acknowledgments

This book is dedicated to all the children who have passed through my dojo. As Master Joe Kelljchian, my beloved instructor, said to me, "the children have taught me so much more than I have taught them." Thank you.

Deep appreciation to the following:

Jackie Kan for her invaluable help in proofreading;

Cynthia Galapon for her expertise in layout and design;

Tracey Broussard for her expertise in publishing

and

All the kids, in all the schools who patiently let us take the pictures.

Table Of Contents

Chapter		Page
1	Introduction	9
2	Techniques for Classroom Management	37
3	Variety of Workouts	83
4	One More Thing	137
5	Seriously! One more thing.	149
	Glossary	154

CHAPTER 1
INTRODUCTION

Welcome!

This book is a compendium of blogposts I wrote and can be found at: *www.kickswithkids.blogspot.com*.

My intention here is to create some thought and even a little debate about how we teach our kids today. These words are specific, but not limited to, karate.

I want to start, as I do when I teach a seminar, by posing this question. What are you trying to accomplish with the time you spend teaching students ranging from age 3 to 13?

And this would be my answer:

I want to create the opportunity for a practitioner to become strong, smart and capable enough to stand up for him (or her) self, while being simultaneously courteous, patient, and self-disciplined enough not to abuse his (or her) skills.

This is a lofty goal by any measure. To accomplish this, I need to know my students for many years. Changes and growth of that proportion won't happen in 6 months or a year. (For those of you who do not know it, I teach in a Japanese system where a student must be 17+ to test for a black belt.). If I can allow karate to influence their lives for 4 to 6 years, they have a chance of attaining strength of body, strength of technique, and strength of character.

Years ago, when I realized that my goal was to keep, influence, and affect students for years, I began thinking how the boring redundancy of old fashioned repetition can cause children to walk away before they have learned the many things that karate has to offer them. (You have probably changed up your teaching routine, just because you got tired of the sameness. Do you know what I mean?)

On these pages we'll explore changes you can try -- changes that can be made without losing the integrity of the *dojo*. I will also detail how teaching kids 3 to 5 years old is significantly different from the students that are 6 to 10 years old. Last, but most difficult, I'll brainstorm ideas on holding the attention of the teens with the attention span of a gnat (unless they are playing video, right?)

Today's thoughts are about general class structure and management: Each one of us has to find our own voice. I like to teach with laughter: without letting the students start talking and joking among themselves and without making jokes at the expense of the students. What works best for you? Try different approaches for example:

- Sometimes let the students copy you and sometimes let them work independent of you.
- Yell to elicit a strong spirit but not to humiliate. Then go immediately to a quiet voice and watch the kids strain to listen and stay with you.
- Be consistent in your discipline. An inconsistent example I see often is a boy and a girl doing the same crime but don't get the same punishment. Fit the punishment to the crime. Remember that pleasing the karate teacher is tantamount to most of these kids. Some of you could be having the opposite

problem (animals running the farm). I can go to that on another post.

- Make breaches in courtesy as important (or more important) than movement mistakes. That will begin the character development of the students.

- When you are in a stand-off with a student over some sort of *dojo* etiquette, try to find a way where you can both win. Try to stay away from the "if / then" type of solution. Instead, try to come up with an idea where the person can choose which destiny he (or she) wants. Here is an example: In our *dojo*, you have to call the sensei "Sensei". A student loses his temper and turns on me and says "yeah". A few assistant instructors correct him by saying "Yes Sensei" and the child stares at me, unyielding. I can say "If you don't say "Yes Sensei you have to do 50 pushups." Or I can say "Johnny, you choose! Say, yes Sensei in any voice you need to and let's all move on, or don't say yes Sensei, do pushups, and then spend the rest of your night mad and bored – it is up to you." The out I gave him was that he could stay in his hostile voice and that the decision was his. I've never had anyone choose not to say the correct words in the incorrect voice. I immediately do something that makes us all do some push ups. Johnny has a chance to get rid of some of his anger with the exercise and we all try again. I will tell you, this one is a little difficult, but it is worth it.

My teacher taught me to teach with dictatorship; that ought to be enough to start some interesting conversations. I welcome questions and comments. Instead of just keeping on punching, let's keep on letting our kids punch!

Pre Class Routine
(January 2011)

Have you ever noticed that what happens before class can set the tone for the hour of training time? I have tried many different routines, but the one I've used for the past few years is to sit everyone in a circle, 10 or 15 minutes before class and talk. Children will talk about anything and everything. They will want to tell you about their day, or the latest movie or an upcoming trip. You never know.

My experience is that by bringing all the kids together before we start training I accomplish four things:

1. Everyone has a chance to drop the distractions in their heads and mentally prepare for training.

2. Kids want to come early to talk and laugh. Therefore (theoretically) I have less late arrivals.

3. Kids LOVE to talk about themselves. (So do we, so we should understand that, right?)

4. Everyone feels inclusive. As kids arrive, they join in. Even new students feel like part of the group before class starts. Some of their first day jitters disappear during this talk

Usually one of my helpers begins the pre class talk time while I'm organizing for class; each teacher has an individual way of coordinating this time. One thing we all agree on is that only one person should talk at a time. That is a challenge.

It comes, like most things in karate, with patience, reminders, and repetition. Recently I had seven new students arrive before class started. I used the pre class talk to have everyone introduce themselves, say how old they are and what grade they are in. I could see the kids noticing when they are in the same grade, or the same age. I realized that bringing up things newcomers and old timers had in common made everyone more comfortable and therefore less distracted at the beginning of training.

One other thing I'll do during talk time is move the conversation over to karate ideas. As we get closer to class time, I'll start asking karate questions and see who remembers what.

That is a perfect segue to the "Line up." Command.

As I stated, I've been using talking in a circle for a few years now. Recently, one of my students, who is a

school teacher, brought in a document from her
Montessori program reinforcing what we had already
seen. Here are a couple of the bullets from her paper.

Bringing kids together to talk in a circle
- *Unifies the group.*
- *Makes everyone feel like they belong.*
- *Lets everyone express themselves and understand what they have in common and how to be friends with differences.*
- *The teacher can use this time to review rules, expectations.*
- *This time is perfect to move from one type of activity to the next.*

Keeping in Touch with Parents
(March 2011)

I always consider myself a work in progress. However, where parent communication is concerned, I'm a slow learner. To make things more complicated, each parent is a person with their own viewpoint, busy schedule, and needs. Therefore, each conversation is slightly different. The only way to know how to individualize the conversation is to be a good listener. Understand what the person is asking and try to answer accordingly.

There are three areas of communication that are worth discussing:

- welcoming newcomers,
- keeping everyone informed
- one on one communications

Welcoming New Students (and their parents)

Recently I sent one of my brown belts to welcome a new child (and his parents). They arrived after the class had begun and I was busy with other things. When adult class started, the brown belt said "Sensei, I have a question. What, exactly, do we say when we're talking to parents on their first day?" Up until that moment, I hadn't really thought a lot about what I say.

Right then, we brainstormed and here is the short list:

The child comes early enough to join the circle time

When the child joins circle I talk to parents.

I say "HI" and thanks for your interest. Next, I introduce myself to the adults and shake hands, etc. Then I put my attention to the child. I bend down and say "Hi". I put my hand out to see if they'll shake and ask their name. If they hide behind their mom's leg, I turn my attention back to the adult and let the child acclimate. At that point I say to the parent, "Johnny may want to just watch today. If he does, that is fine. Then next time he comes he can have his try out."

At that point I bend down to Johnny once again and repeat the sentence. I show everyone to their seat and say to Johnny. "If you decide to come and join us, just get my attention."

(Traveling back to the moment when I introduce myself to the child) If the child shakes my hand and tells me his name I say to him, "Would you like to try the class today. We're probably going to have fun." Hopefully all this is happening before class starts. In my dojo, before class starts, we all sit together and talk about everything and anything. Shy or outgoing, at this point I say to the child "Would you like to sit with us and talk? We're talking about video games, movies, favorite sport, whatever! Most children can't resist the chance to talk. As you all know, we train without shoes. However, if the child seems shy, I DON'T mention their shoes at this point. If they seem comfortable, I say "Would you like to take off your shoes now?"

On the child's first day, whether they wear shoes or not, it isn't a deal breaker. Some children need more time to acclimate to the room before they trust enough to do anything they think is unusual.

It all seems like common sense until you're standing there without backup trying to figure out what to do and say. As the parents are sitting and watching, I take a moment during the class to drop off a small packet with "Parent Information" in it. This packet contains a list of parent conduct I appreciate:

This consists of:
1. *A signup sheet*
2. *A list of my locations and times*
3. *A fee sheet*

4. *A sheet that asks parents to watch quietly, take phone calls and conversations outside.*
5. *A sheet that explains that taking pictures is allowed.*
6. *And finally a sheet that asks parents to make their habit to communicate with me outside of training time when possible because that 60 minute period is so busy that fitting conversation with parents in is distracting for me. I encourage my parents to email. But lots of them text and a few like to talk on the phone. I've been thinking that some of you might not agree with this. You might like to deal with parents ONLY during training time and I would love to hear how you balance the time. I don't like missing time with the kids and I like missing my adult class even less. So talking to parents AFTER class is even more uncomfortable for me. What are your thoughts?*

Keeping Parents Informed

When I was a karate student, hard copy flyers were the only means of communication with students and parents. Although I use that method, I prefer to email parents with a flyer on an upcoming event. Parents like this too. I have a group of parents in my address book. Anytime I get a new student, I add the parents' name to the group and send them a "Welcome" email. I send flyers on competitions, seminars, extra workouts, etc. Since I send all information on the computer it encourages questions via email rather than in class. I've also found that less people take flyers in class, telling me they already have one at home! Do you all use this method? I also use the computer to remind parents if their fee is due. I have really good luck with this. Let me know what you all do? On a personal note: I NEVER forward to parents. I don't think it is professional to fill their box with junk. I also think that distracts from the information I'd really like them to notice when they see my email address in their "in" box.

I'd like to close this post with a quote that an education instructor once told me and it has been unquestionably the most helpful tool I've had in working with parents:

"Remember, when you're talking to parents, that every one of them is doing the best they can with what they have to work with at that moment in time."

Working with Children (and Parents) Individually (April 2011)

In the last post I opened the door to the idea that with children students, comes parent communication. Does this come easily to you? Have you tried any new ideas? Something that happens to me on a regular basis is that a parent will come to me with an individual problem with their child. Some examples include: his or her grades are falling, the respect level around the house is becoming too relaxed, or maybe they are fighting in school. Do your parents ever approach you for help in an individual area?

The pattern for working through these requests is manageable, yet a little time consuming. First, I set up a meeting with the child. This can be before, during, or after class. The time I pick depends on how much time I think the meeting will take. My least favorite is during class. I will pick it if I have enough help and it is the best alternative given the circumstances. Before I call the child in, I mention to the parent that I am going to talk to the child. I say that I would appreciate it if they listen quietly and let me lead the conversation. I tell them that before we close, I'll ask them if they have anything to add, but during the talk I'd like them to let the child talk directly with me – without any interruptions. Most parents understand, agree, and comply.

I find a quiet spot for the three (or four if mom and dad are both there) of us to sit. I ask the student if they know why we're meeting. Almost half say 'yes' and we get right to it. The other half like to say no and we have to identify the behavior we're going to work on before we can talk about it.

Three things I've noticed about the meeting are quite simple and repeatable:

1. Since the child loves karate, he (or she) will try to do what I ask.
2. The method for change in any of us is the same.
3. Finish with the part of the conversation where mom and dad can add what they want. They inevitably muddy the conversation with lots of emotion. I quietly wait. Then I reiterate the bullets I want in behavior and we all go back to class (or home).

The Child Loves Karate (1)

Parents are always enthralled at how well behaved their child is in class. They always want to take the concept of push-ups at home to demand good behavior. We all know that doesn't work. We also know that the reason, the children do what we ask is because these children love having the strengthening outlet of a fighting art. It is a magnificent teacher and a great equalizer. When I'm working with kids to change their behavior, I try to stay away from "if-then" demands. In other words I try to stay away from sentences like "If you want to become a green belt, then you will finish your homework on time." What I like instead is to let the person come to the place where they think it is what they should do.

It goes something like this:

Me: Do you know why we're talking?

Child: Mom is mad because I don't ever want to do my homework?

Me: Way to go! Saying it right up front. Do you have something to add before I talk? Is your homework too hard for you? Is there a problem we don't know about?

(If there is a problem, we brainstorm ways to fix it – tutors, talking to the teacher, bringing the work into karate to get some help with the overwhelming parts?)

Otherwise-

Child: No, I just think it is boring!

Me (smiling): I know what you mean! Let's talk about why you have to do it (and we do). Now let's talk about how to make the time work for you (and we do). And finally, let's talk about how a karate person thinks…does a karate person quit when the work gets hard? Does a karate person whine and make excuses?

At this point, I let the child talk and consider. Then we discuss the tools we're going to use to change. I finish with "Can you give me your word as a karate person that you will TRY to do your best?" (I reiterate the "try your best" promise at the very end of our meeting)

I expect setbacks. It usually goes great for about two weeks and then we have a setback. I have a conversation with mom and dad where I mention to allow for setbacks and try not to overreact. Just remind, and I will too. (I have three or four children giving me weekly updates on how they're doing with the parent's requests even as I write this!)

Method of Change (2)

What I have observed over the years is that no matter what age, everyone needs motivation to change. Otherwise, a person really won't consciously try to change. I have also observed that there are a few ways to actually change: you can replace one behavior with another, give yourself a reminder when you are about to do something you don't want to do, or reward yourself when you get it right! These 'methods of changing' remain the same throughout life.

One thing I think is very important, is to give the child the tools to attempt the change. In the above example of homework, the obvious tool is to make the same time for homework each day. Have an alarm go off for starting and one go off, if there are breaks scheduled etc. I would make sure the homework time wasn't falling into the child's favorite show or the time his friend was playing a game outside, in other words, look at it from their standpoint. I also believe in small rewards. **This is controversial because I'm sure some of you 'old-schoolers' are reading this and saying -"People should work and do without constant reward".**

Theoretically you are SO right. Realistically, animals and people learn faster and change more consistently when the reminders are in place. **Rewards don't have to be big or dramatic. I like to use things the** kids are getting already: new games, favorite videos rented. I have used events like they could earn an archery lesson

with me or I would let them earn patches…etc. It is very
individual.)

Some other tools I have used include:

- Making lists when needed
- Reinforcing when the kids get it right and not
  just noticing when they get it wrong. (This is
  probably the most common mistake we make
  when we're working to change ourselves or
  someone we care for. The successes become
  invisible to the eye. But the mistakes stand out.
  It is hard to notice when people do something
  right. But it is worth it to make an effort to
  notice; in ourselves and in our children.)
- Creating a way for the person to see disaster
  coming. One example is a "secret word"
  between the adult and the child to signal when
  the child is getting agitated. I like silly words
  that other people won't recognize, like dinosaur

or power puffs. That gives the person a chance to breathe and think before all heck breaks loose.

- <u>Making sure the children have an outlet to vent.</u> Everyone needs that. Many people do it in a social network now. For a child it could be the parent, a teacher, a grandparent. We are a society that needs to be heard.
- <u>Finally, a conversation</u> I have regularly with kids includes the concept that we can't lash out at everyone who gets on our nerve (even if we want to). When someone, or something, gets on our nerve, we need to choose between these alternatives: walk away from it, talk about it, ignore it, or tell someone who can help. I stress that physicality is only for emergencies. I also stress the idea that the four choices above travel with you throughout life, so get used to them!

Mom and Dad Talk and Listen (3)

When the meeting is about to close up, I ask moms and/or dads what they'd like to add. This is always laced with emotion. I sit quietly and observe. When it gets quiet, I ask the child to share. I will also reiterate the bullets from our conversation. We put this subject to rest and go about the rest of the evening.

After I send the child away, I mention to the parents that change is really challenging. I ask them to consider what it would be if THEY were the ones being expected to adapt. I try to finish on a note of win-win.

Here is a comprehensive list of subjects that have been brought before me. It is not complete, just ones I remember:

1. Hitting and bullying other kids.
2. Being hit and bullied.
3. Not respecting parents.
4. Acting up during divorce.
5. Not doing home chores.
6. Not doing homework.
7. Not wanting to spend weekends with the other parent because the child had to miss his / her regular weekend event.

Hopefully, this post is helpful when and if you find yourself in moment where a parent asks for your help.

Cause I'm Bigger than You
(March 2012)

A couple of years ago, I was standing in one of my schools and I heard the student ask the teacher why he had to do something. She responded with the title words, "Cause I'm bigger than you." In defense of the teacher, let's agree that sometimes we can all be flippant and impatient with students. Because I'm asked to have specific conversations with children about their behaviors in class and at home, I've put quite a bit of time into thinking about the most effective way to communicate with them. I've noticed some interesting truths. Even if you aren't asked to talk to kids about their attitude and choices outside the dojo, you might find my experience and the resulting conclusions interesting.

Talking at Kids

Often I'll watch an adult command a child and the adult isn't even looking at the child. The exchange goes something like this: Adult "Stop spinning, Johnny!" The child stops, then starts again. By time the adult turns to look, it appears as if the child didn't stop. Confusion begins already! I know we're busy. I know we're trying to get a lot done in our time with our students. My thought is only that we take time to actually BE with the students. Use all our senses - eyes, ears, and intuition - to create a strong environment for growth. I remind myself often that my students are much more likely to become what I show them than what I tell them. Students will emulate what we are.

What We Say / What They Hear

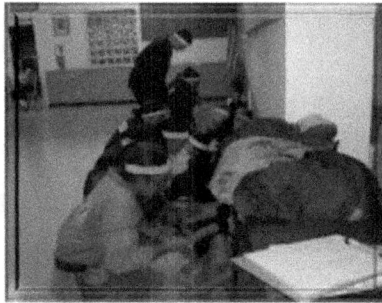

Keeping their Attention

One of the biggest complaints I have from teachers is that "Johnny doesn't listen."
(So much so that I made a little song to help the kids remember. Link : http://www.youtube.com/channel/UCM-9YgtyMHLWxTihpMsfdOg)

Johnny would inevitably say "I'm listening, Sensei." I couldn't see why it wasn't working, so I watched and listened to the dynamic. I realized that the adult wasn't being clear. She wanted the child to listen AND do what she asked. (In a best case, do it the First time she asked!) But that isn't what she said. Once I started explaining to the children that they not only had to listen, they had to "do what the teacher says", things began to slowly change. The children really tried and the teachers learned that they weren't being clear. You might see this happen in your dojo or your classroom. I have and I've really listened to myself to make sure I was clear in my directions. It has been interesting and helpful both inside and outside the dojo.

The Words Themselves

Two great teachers at work

I'm going to stay on the example I was just using. In that same conversation the teacher would say, in utter frustration, "Johnny won't follow directions!" I turn to Johnny and say "What does it mean to follow directions?" Johnny says "To be good." Smiling I would say (over and over in as calm a tone as I can) "It means to do what the teacher asks you to do." I would have Johnny say it back to me. Slowly he would begin to change. We all grew from that simple exchange. The child, myself and the teacher are all smarter, better communicators, and better listeners from that event.

An Old Karate Saying

When I received my first degree black belt and my teacher was talking to me about how to treat students, he said, "With one side of your hand demand from the student. With the other side of your hand earn their respect." This stayed with me over the years. (The application when training adults is more subtle and possibly more physical.) However, where kids are concerned, I interpret this to mean that the children need to do what I say, when I say it. Simultaneously I am also there 100%: working, caring, looking; I am an active member of the training process. In this dynamic, both of the parameters above are met.

Sometimes, during training, I stop and explain <u>why</u> I want things a certain way. This may be an unusual trait, as I have had more than one teacher and parent mention to me that they have adopted the technique after observing it.

Two situations brought me to this idea of making sure that children had an opportunity to understand why I make the decisions I make.

1. I noticed confusion on the faces of students. The look made me stop and empathize with them. What would it feel like if someone twice as big as I am was barking at me without giving me a minute to understand?

2. Sometimes a student that is a little more courageous will question <u>why</u> he should do a certain thing. Because I want him (or her)

to leave stronger, more confident, and more respectful than when he (or she) arrived. In order for a young person to grow in respect, adults need to make a little sense. SO..... I began to think, when time allowed, a little explanation would go a long way. (Compare that to adult training where technology is the most important thing; individual moods and attitudes are [at best] secondary.)

One of the first times I remember explaining was when a fourth grade student asked why we do extra push-ups (aka punishment push-ups). As I explained, the look on the child's face as he began to understand was priceless. An unintentional surprise was how wonderful it felt to clarify the concept in my thoughts as I was explaining. I knew why, but saying it aloud gave me clarity that was previously not there – an excellent example of the teacher learning more than the student.

Many times since then I've stopped training a small group to explain everything from what muscle group gets stronger with what exercise to why we bow. I use intuition to distinguish between a child with a real inquiry and a student who is talking to be disrespectful, rude, or lazy.

Just recently I was teaching two brand new little guys (4 and 5 years old). We were starting kata and I asked them if they knew what 'memorize' meant. One said "Oos Sensei, it means to forget." I smiled at that response. After a quick back and forth about remembering something for a long time, we began our work.

Sensei Harrison having fun with the kyus

The point, of course, is that our goal should be to create a population that will grow up courageous enough to do whatever is necessary each day, while, simultaneously producing men and women that are genuinely respectful. I can only see this happening in an atmosphere where respect and responsibility are mutual and communication clear. It is challenging to remain 'fresh' in our attitude day after day and year after year. For me one way to keep teaching fresh is to remember that, like my students, I am a work in progress.

CHAPTER 2
Techniques for Classroom Management

Tip:

Watch the eyes of your students. You can tell right away when students are saturated with technology, when they don't understand the words you are using, when they are glued to your energy and ready for more.

Keep An Eye On The Eyes.

Here you can see Yoli keeping an eye on Stephanie's eyes.

Using Assistant Karate Teachers
(July 2009)

Here is one possible use of assistant teachers.

You have 20 kids. The ranks are 5 beginners, 3 are 7th kyu, 5 are 6th kyu, 2 at 5th kyu, 2 at 4th, and 3 are 3rd through 1st kyu.

Set the workout to run all the way to the end of class. Have your assistant take out the small groups quietly. He / she should drop kids back in and remove new ones without interrupting the flow of the class. (The first time you are going to do this, tell the children what you are doing so that they are ready to walk away from the group quietly and THEN turn and do the courtesy bow to you. This will allow you to keep the flow going.)

The helper should start by figuring out how much time to spend with each group. If they begin 5 minutes after class starts, and go to 10 minutes before class ends, they will have 45 minutes for 6 groups. That will give them a little more than 5 minutes per group. They have to hustle. I suggest the individual instructor start with the 'brown' belts (3 – 1 kyu). You and your helper need to decide in advance what technology each rank should be working on. It flows well. He or she will keep trading one group for the next. The time will fly.

Sensei Jackie is helping one student, while the others work in the background.

Meanwhile, you have an hour long class set up in your head. Of course, you can start with a few minutes of meditation. Then do 15 minutes of stretch and exercise and another 10 minutes on stances, blocking, striking and history. Then you can go to bag work, or self defense or kata basics for another 10 – 15 minutes.

Now it is time to spar, with just enough time to do meditation and announcements before bowing out.

This class structure works really well. If your helper comes on time, you can have him / her run the class while YOU look at individual growth and technology.

Now that I have given you a structure to try in your dojo (Let me know how it works.), I would like to talk a little about how to get more people to show up as helpers.

Here are some ideas that have worked for me:

Take a minute in adult class to:

Talk about the benefits of coming in early and helping. Remind them that they will master ONLY through teaching. Publicly recognize the people who showed up and helped. ("Thanks to John and Sally for showing up and helping")

Spend a minute at the beginning of adult class talking about what worked and what didn't work when they were working with the kids. That will make the other students care.

In this shot, I am going over a chasing game with some instructors

Take a minute at the end of kid's class to:

Have the kids thank the assistant teachers that aren't black belts. Give them their props.

Finally and most importantly actually USE the helpers that do show up. That means that occasionally you won't get to run the show. They get to warm up class (see below), be in charge of the end of the day event / sparring / whatever it is, and teach something other than blocking and Tekkie 1. It took me a few years before I became even slightly comfortable managing helpers instead of running class. It was a big change for me, but a huge plus for the children to have small work groups with a teacher instead of being lost in a sea of kids who already know the material.

In my dojo, these days, it is unusual for me to have only one helper and even more rare for me to be alone. I make it a point to give the helpers teaching jobs that will let them grow. I take on the hard to teach students myself. I use my peripheral vision to watch the other groups and give my helpers pointers on how to keep the kids attention or use words that the kids will understand when I notice they had a problem. I always thank my helpers for showing up.

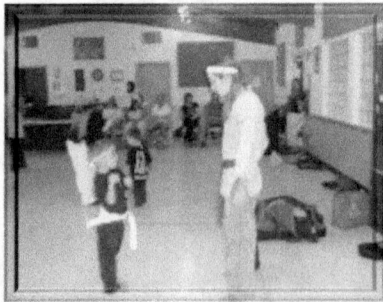

Four groups working at the same time

So here is the bottom line:

To get helpers you are going to need to encourage them, motivate them, thank them and give them jobs that challenge them (not like in the old days when we sat and waited for Sensei to give us a job, remember that?) Everyone wins when adults show up for the kid's class. The adults are pumped for their class, already warmed up, the kids get the attention they need and attach themselves to people other than you. (That is awesome the first few times you see it, by the way.) Last, and very importantly, you are free to see the big picture and figure out where to go from here. Please let me know how this works out for you.

Kata and the word "No"
(August 2009)

Here is a challenge for all of us: Watch yourself teach kata – either in group or individually – How often do you start your corrections with the word "no".

(The sentence looks something like this: "No, use the other hand." Or "No, you were supposed to double stomp there." Or "No, you weren't supposed to double stomp there." You get the idea.)

After having watched children's eyes for years now, I've decided that starting my corrections with the word "no" is negatively distracting to them. It seems so obvious, doesn't it? However, try as I might, it is a habit I find hard to break!

Here are a few other choices to try instead of starting with the word "no".

1. Looks good so far, I want you to try this.
2. Alright, let's start again and when I say the word 'stop' - freeze right there so we can try something.
3. Hold on; switch your hands, oos?
4. Let's do it again and this time, just copy me. (My favorite)

Have you ever noticed that when kids are really young, 6 and under, they have a lot of trouble telling their left from their right. (So do I, maybe that is why I noticed.) I put a sticker on their left hand so they don't have to manage which hand is which AND my corrections!

44

Here, Anthony and I both have stickers on our left hand while practicing a form.

Kata training is a large part of traditional karate training. Peter Urban mentions in his book, The Karate Dojo, that a practitioner is drawn to either sparring or kata, but not usually both. I always try to break that stereotype myself, and get my students to break it. This creates the challenge of making kata training a little interesting. One easy way to do that is to let students build their own kata. I like to put that into lessons that are near the holidays. Since the classes are small (because everyone is busy), it is a great time to try something creative.

Below you will find a few more variations on how to play with kata. (For those of you who prefer it, we can say "work kata".) Let me know if you see a difference in how the kids react to kata training after trying a few of these ideas.

Do you agree with this statement: When teaching kata to kids you have to divide the work into two big categories?

1. The moves of the kata in the right order.
2. The details. Details include stances, gaze control, breathing, chamber hand and fighting spirit, in no particular order. This photo shows Sensei Jackie working with some beginners on moves in the right order.

When I am working with a group of students, some who know the kata and some who are learning it, the first thing I do is move the experienced people to the four outside corners of the group so the beginners can copy.

This photo shows purple belts leading a group learning their first kata.

I tell the students what my plan is. Including the kids in this puts the new ones at ease and makes the children who know the moves feel important. The children who are being copied will work harder knowing they are an example. While we are practicing the kata moves, I will give extra corrections to the kids who know the moves. Another important thing I have learned to do is use less words, almost just 'cues' to describe the moves. I have found that while the kids are moving AND listening, using too many words causes them to get lost. Also, with 'cue' words, I can give them hints when they forget moves and let them come to the information on their own. If you want a few examples, write me.

After 3 - 5 times through the kata, the children start to lose interest. One way to change things up it to switch to using sticks to mean "do the next move".

This will do a few things:

    1. It will cause the kids to prick up their ears and listen again.

2. You can use your words for corrections, and the kids will be able to differentiate between the command to move and a correction.

Finally, after a few times using sticks, I like to divide the group into "those that know the moves and those that are learning". I let one group do it from beginning to end, trying to stay together while group 2 watches. When group two does the kata, I give them reminders using the 'cue' words along the way. This photo shows the advanced group watching the beginners do the form with me.

A variation on this 'game' (or drill if you prefer that term) goes like this: After I divide the kids into "old timers and newer kids" I sit one group down to watch the other. With the new kids we do a review of moves in the right order. With the more experienced group I play the game where they only move if I say the right term. For example I might say 'break' when their eyes are still closed. Then I will say block instead of strike. Those that move do just a couple of push-ups. I don't give 10 push-ups to kids in this game because I want them to like the game and want to play again. Also, it is important to me that the kids learn to tell themselves the truth. It is easy for me to get them to want to take responsibility for their actions if the price is only two push-ups. Everyone has fun, laughs, and wants to 'do it again'. Leaving the kids wanting more is exactly what I am after.

The above workout is about 12 or 15 minutes long. That is about the amount of time kids age 6-12 can concentrate on one subject. (Children younger than 6 have a much shorter attention span.)

Here are a few more thoughts on teaching kata:

Of course we need to emphasize both group kata and individual kata. Have you ever considered why it is important to do both?

Group kata is important because the practitioner needs to be willing to compartmentalize his / her ego for the group to perform well. I'd like to say this is harder for kids than adults. However, my experience is that it is difficult for all of us and that when a person is good at group kata, individual kata is more challenging and vice versa. To me this emphasizes the importance of both. Don't forget to let kids make up their own kata. That drill is great at holiday time. Everyone puts on a show of their kata at the end of the class. Kids are inventive and the creativity can't be beat.

Tone of Voice
(May 2012)

I observed something one day that caused me to stop and write this. I'd like to start by telling you the point of the story:

We all need to be aware of the power of our voice. If we use the same tone all the time, then we run the risk of being dismissed and ignored. We have both a loud and quiet voice as well as many tones we can use, if only we remember. (Examples of different tones are: serious, playful, really mad and the distracted). And we have the look in our eyes.

How we use them with our students is going to affect how the relationship grows and changes.

Now, for the back story:

I walked into one of my schools and a teacher said one of my students was biting. I sat with the student to talk about what happened and what to do instead of biting. The teacher was sitting with me. As I was talking and listening to my student the teacher constantly interjected in a yelling voice: "Do you hear her? You are in real trouble. You had better listen and change."

Finally, I asked the teacher to leave us alone and I finished with my student. We discussed alternative choices when you are frustrated. We also discussed consequences if things remained the same. (I used kid friendly words rather than the grown up ones.) I haven't had a problem since.

Lastly, I went to the teacher one on one and tried to discuss not to yell all the time. It did not go well, because she was yelling! I accepted that no change would come today and moved on.

I know this isn't the most exciting post. But the point is important: We need to build respect and trust while we command and demand. **We need to remember that our students are going to become what we are, not what we tell them to be** (no matter how loud we say it!). Even though we are all experienced, it is easy to let the distractions of classroom management get in the way of our tone with the children. I figured we could all use this reminder.

Start Each Day Fresh
(September 2010)

As summer turned into the school year, I observed a few teaching styles that I'd like to list and comment on.

One thing I really remind myself of often is to start each day fresh with the children. If I have a really tough discipline/courtesy day with a student, it is a test of strength for me to start fresh the next day. It is, however, imperative for the growth of the student to give them another chance to do better. It is important that I not be one of those teachers that label students. I would like to hear from you on this one. Do you find this challenging too?

A second observation of late is the importance of being a little organized before I arrive in class. When I was a teacher alone, with just a few students, it wasn't so important. Now I have larger classes, these classes run from beginners to advanced, and I have adults who want to be trained as assistant instructors. With all that happening in only an hour, a small game plan helps.

Here is an example:

At the start of the week, I think about what is happening in the dojo (testing, competitions, what technology I have and have not covered lately) and I make a general game plan. If possible, I share it with my helpers.

As an example I might say to them, "I need to put time into stances this week, and I haven't played fire-rope in a while. Sound good?" Then, I make sure I have everything I need with me.

Another example: "Today I'm going to do team sparring. If we finish in time, we'll exercise at the end of class."

On a related note, I'll finish this section with a quick story. Often, parents will ask me to talk to the kids about school and home behavior. Recently, I was working with a little girl on not pouting when she doesn't get her way. We talked about what pouting is. I even pretended to show it, so she could see it. Then I ask her to try not to pout this week. When her mom picked her up, and she didn't get her way, she immediately started pouting. I thought about it later, and realized I had left out one important ingredient in the conversation - giving her a suggestion of what to do **instead** of pouting. The next time I saw her, I said "I was thinking that instead of pouting you could say 'I'm sad, but I'll try to wait and not pout. ok?' Try that, ok?" She complained a little. In our hour together she got a little practice. I have seen her since and she is doing better with each try. The point is that **she needed a plan** on what to do instead of what she was doing that wasn't working.

Another example of the same thing is seen in how I talk to the kids about not hitting or pushing other kids when they get frustrated. I say to them "Instead of hitting, this is what we should do - walk away, tell the teacher, talk it over, or just ignore them." That way these kids have a better choice to achieve what we're asking them to do.

Two notes on that last example:

1. Sometimes, if I have a little extra time I play a game where we bother each other and try to ignore it, so kids can learn what ignoring something is.

2. If you think about it, the choices we give the kids are the same ones we have to learn to live with.

Balancing Opposites
(October 2011)

The three opposites I'll address here are Compliments and Criticism, If / Then, and of *Go / Ju.*

Compliments and Criticism

Have you ever watched the faces of the children when you are teaching or judging them? Do you see their faces light up when you give them the smallest compliment? Do you use the methodology of placing your corrections in between some words of encouragement? A black belt recently mentioned that he thought students were getting weaker. I would like to offer an opposite view. Maybe children aren't weaker. Here are three ideas on that subject:

1. Our memories are based on the difficulties we overcame as kyus. However, if I really look back, I have many memories of my Sensei giving me encouragement. I have memories of him believing in me more than I believed in myself.

2. The saying "I do to my students what was done to me" isn't necessarily the healthiest teaching style. Unless you have a photographic and objective memory, it is possible that what was "done to you" was much more complicated than you remember. A few people do have photographic memories. I don't know anyone who judges their own past objectively. Most of us are quite subjective.

3. The student grows to admire the Sensei in a way that borders on worship. There is such a responsibility on the part of a Sensei to properly manage that trust. If all we do is correct and criticize the student verbally, and they don't have a great self-image, we need to think if we are partially responsible for that.

I am not asking teachers to lie to students and tell them they're great when they're not. I'm asking you to include empathy in your teaching style. Think about how it feels to constantly be corrected without compliments or encouragement to balance out the work.

Here is a (hopefully) quick example. I have a 6 year old who cannot hold still OR be quiet. We're working on it. At a few points during the training I will turn to him and mention that I see he is holding still (or holding his words in). He beams at the compliment.

One last opinion: Keep your mind open for something to say to everyone within the training time.

Please don't be a person who only compliments the physically talented students and doesn't notice the effort of the majority of the students. Oos?

If / Then

I sometimes wonder if I am the only teacher who has students with self-control issues. I cannot imagine I am. We all know the standard ways to work through these. Here are a few I use regularly:

1. Remind the kids before class of your expectations.
2. Redirect their attention during training.
3. Keep them busy.
4. Be a good example.
5. Give them incentive.
6. Ignore the indiscretion.

(Reminders and incentives are subjects I am interested in, yet there is no room in this post to go into detail. Write me if this is something you have ideas, questions, or opinions about.)

What I want to discuss here is the waste of effort in the use of the words IF / THEN. First let me give you an example.

Teacher to student: "If you interrupt me again, I'm not going to let you spar."

This creates a lose/lose situation. The reason this is lose / lose is because you have created an adversarial relationship with someone you are trying to mentor. Also, in karate, we're trying to raise people who are willing to step up to a challenge and now we've created a negative challenge. How could it surprise us when they step to the challenge?

There are many ways to figure out how to handle this kind of situation. Write me and tell me what works for you. I'll tell you a couple of strategies that I like. (I'm going to use the example of kids talking during training. But the strategy will work for other interruptions.):

1. Especially if it is sound related, I'll stop training for a second and address the comment. ("I'm thirsty!" is an example.) Then I'll say "Does everyone agree we should get back to training? "We'll finish this and then all get water?" And we'll go back to it.

2. If someone interrupts again with the same problem, I'll say "Would you guys rather do that than get to the end of the day game that I planned?" Sometimes people ask" what is the game today?" I smile and say I won't tell. Everyone agrees we should get back to work.

3. With a really young class (ages 5 to 7) I have situations where the student wouldn't or couldn't control him (or her) self. Here is my first choice in that situation. If I am alone, I get the class repeating a movement to a sound (usually music). While they're moving and the music is noisy, I go over and privately ask the child if he thinks he can start to control the behavior. He almost always says yes and we push on. (Then I

notice and say good job as we continue.) If I have helpers, I let a helper teach. Take the child and ask him if he thinks he can control the action, join us and have fun. I try not to seem impatient. The child usually says yes. We go back and I use the compliment when I can. I also compliment after class when I can.

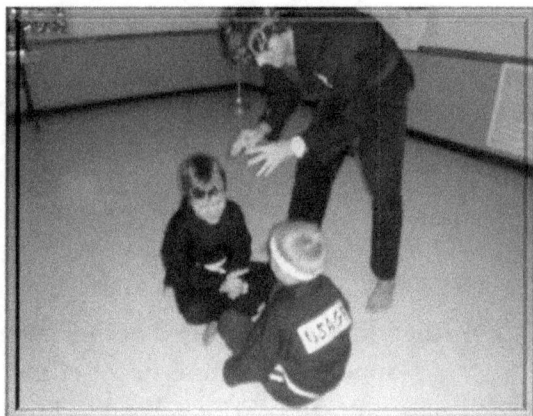

4.   I ignore it. I have an entire game where I teach my kids to ignore annoying distractions. In the game, they sit and talk to each other and the teachers are the annoying people. The children's job is to ignore the annoyance completely. Don't look up, react to it, or address it in any way. It is tricky, fun and a great learning experience.

The thing I try to remember daily is that I am trying to make a student who is strong, confident, self-disciplined and courteous.

I'm not trying to make a mini-me. I'm trying to make a magnificent Them.

To close off this portion of the post, I want to relate a story a parent told me. One of my students wanted to go to a karate summer camp. I said "Go. Have fun!" A few days after camp started, the mom came to me and said she pulled her son out of camp. The camp Sensei came to her at the end of the day and told her that her son was "a tough nut to crack" but she would do it! To me this is a perfect example of a Sensei who doesn't really understand that the job of the Sensei is to create a great individual, NOT squish out all traces of individuality.

Needless to say, the young man was ready to leave when mom suggested it.

A busy room, working and growing

Go / Ju

This last little discussion isn't really about kids. It is just about opposites creating the whole. Of course *Go* means hard and *Ju* means soft. That is the style of Martial Art I study. Many of us talk about balancing hard and soft.

Examples abound:
- courtesy and fighting spirit,
- exertion and meditation,
- work and play

However, I'm interested in the idea that teachers still mistake kindness for weakness <u>in themselves</u>. The saying "Don't mistake kindness for weakness" was told to me by my teacher many years ago. It is one of those sentences that is easy to say, but elusive to live by. I encourage you to look closely. Call upon your kindness and notice that when you call upon something it originates in your chi line. Therefore, because of its origin, it is powerful. Then, you might notice, the next time you call upon your chi to say "no" it will be more powerful, confident, and less reactionary.

Teaching Kids / Teaching Adults
(October 2012)

One of the beautiful things about being a Karate teacher is that my youngest student is 3 years old and my oldest student is....well, old enough to be revered. In comparing the two types of classes, I realized that a couple of trite sayings really define the making of a great kid's teacher: "Don't phone it in." and "Be in the moment."

This stream of consciousness reminded me that one of the biggest differences in teaching kids and adults is this: In the adult class the technology rules the class. If students bring in a mood or an injury – we push on through and focus on the class content.

However, in a children's class, the children need to be the most important thing, even at the cost of not getting everything done. At least 50% of the time, I'll forfeit some of the content I have planned because there is a subject that needs addressing. Ready or not, it takes some of the training time. That interruption could be anything from hitting each other without Sensei's watchful eye making it safe to fear of something new I'm going to try, to a completely discourteous attitude. In any situation like that I need to stop rushing through the technology. I need to mentally go to where the kids are, allow them to understand my concept, and then be able to carry all of us together to the next thing.

Another difference between training my adults and training my kids is that I rarely plan what the adults will do in advance. When I see the class, I figure out who is there, what they need, and how many teachers I have to accomplish it. Then we do it. **I plan the children's classes a week at a time.** I always know what katas people are learning and what level of self-defense students are on. What I switch often is how we warm up and what we do at the end of class.

It often happens that I have to adjust the plan constantly even as I am teaching. This is easy to say, but doing it is challenging. I'll use my last two nights as examples:

In a class that usually has 10 kids and 3 teachers (I'm spoiled), I had 17students and one helper. Instead of dividing into work groups, (my original plan), I kept the group together with my helper in charge. I took out the most experienced students. I worked on their level of technology and then had them help teach the younger students. This isn't rocket science, I know, but it did entail thinking on my feet. What that means is that I needed to clear the baggage from my head, and quickly think of how to BEST take care of EVERYONE in the room.

The next night I normally have 15 children and 3 teachers. Due to a storm we had 10 children and 5 teachers. Everyone was 'antsy' because of the stormy weather. I dropped my original plan (standard warm up, kata groups, and sparring) and told the kids we'd start the day with their favorite game. We did. Then I said when they go out to their teacher they'd need to give as much energy to their work as they did to the game. They did! We continued like that: play with punching bags / work technology/ play with blockers/ work memorized movements until we did our final game. For that I mixed two games together (because they requested one and I wanted to spar). I had never mixed group jump rope and sparring before, but hoped it would work. It was great! We used my group jump rope and when you ran out you ran directly into an adult sparring partner.

Again. This wasn't overwhelming. However, I needed to BE THERE and see what we were about IN THE MOMENT. I needed to remember what I wanted to accomplish but have alternative ways to get it done. The challenge with adults is so different. They'll adapt to the technology offered. The saying goes that when you bow into the training area (dojo) you leave your troubles and ego at the door. Children don't know that. Adults (even teachers) aren't perfect at it. I'm lucky to be able to teach both because they complement one another. Children keep me grounded and living in the now and adults challenge me with their desire to understand the way of karate.

Kids as Geniuses
(May 2012)

Here are some interesting comments on my last post.
From Sensei Mel:

"Your observations on how people teach and communicate are so, on point! As you observed, many teachers don't communicate their thoughts clearly, especially to children. When teaching children, I tend to become a child, in thought. I've seen teachers, not just in the dojo, where they speak in vocabulary words way beyond the comprehension of young children. When I bring up a word, let's say like, "noble." I asked them their perception of what the word means. Then we take it from there. The one pet peeve I have when it comes to teaching, is my intolerance for sarcasm. I really don't find a place for it in teaching both children and adults. It undermines our goals for virtues. It can cause confusion in commands being given, as well as ideas and concepts. Worst of all, you really don't want children emulating that behavior being learned in the dojo. When we keep our karate and our concepts "pure" in the way we teach them, it shows in the way the advanced kyus teach it to the beginners."

It is literally impossible for these little guys to be
as big as Sensei Harrison. He is a great example
of bringing karate to their level.

I whole-heartedly agree with Sensei Mel.

In a course I published a little over a decade ago, I said (and still stand by) in 10 years 90% of the kids we teach will have left the dojo and forgotten a large percentage of the technology we taught them. But they will never forget you (or me), the teacher. We represent so much more than an influence. Try to go back to the beginning of your training and think of how you saw your Sensei. Some adjectives that seem on point are talented, powerful, dangerous yet patient, and indefatigable. Many people who read this blog may still idolize their Sensei, while others have traveled far beyond that and have grown to love their teacher as a person; idiosyncrasies and human foibles included. If you aren't a Martial Artist in training, think of the character of teachers you admire. No matter what your individual experience, your teacher's opinion matters. When we are off-handed, condescending, or just plain rude, it affects students in ways we may not realize. Another maxim that I included in that first course all those years ago is this:

"Your students will become what you are, not what you tell them to become."

This brings me to the feedback from Sensei Mark S. He is a principal in a school in FL. He sent a quote they use in his school by a man named John Herner:

"If a child doesn't know how to read... we teach.

If a child doesn't know how to swim... we teach.

If a child doesn't know how to multiply... we teach.

If a child doesn't know how to behave... we punish (rarely works)."

Interesting, don't you think? Again, I'd like to add some comments:

I'm not advocating no punishment. I've talked about win-win / repetition / choices et al in many posts. Here is a short version: If I want my kids to be able to hold still, I need to be able to hold still. (I often laugh with my students about how hard this one is!)

- How handy is balance and forethought in dealing with behavior?
- If I constantly tell someone that they are useless, they will definitely agree with me and fulfill that reality. (Fill in untalented, rude, weak, or stupid where I wrote useless.)
- Conversely, I have seen children grow from gawky, uncoordinated pre-teens into very talented black belts. Black belts that will achieve the ultimate compliment to their teacher and rise to greatness that I have not achieved. I have also

seen kids pass on through the rude stage, the not listening stage, they can't keep their hands to their self-stage….all because I didn't give up on them.

I talk (1 on 1) about behavior

- So much of a karate teacher's job is to repeat something in a voice that makes it sound fresh and then wait for the student to make that concept their own.

Now to finish by addressing the idea that we need kids to see themselves as they really are, use tough love, and make them tow the line. Those of you, who know me, may be surprised to find that I agree with this! The only stipulation I want to add is this: Does it all have to happen at the same time, on the same day, to every person. Is it a huge weakness to let the discombobulated child think that I see talent hidden there and have the patience to wait for it to surface?

If I continue to punish Johnny for interrupting class with unrelated comments, but leave out the humiliating references, and always give him plenty of chances to get it right, if I notice when he does get it right by walking by and saying "I saw that you wanted to make a joke and you held it in. Way to go!" Is that weak teaching skill, or individualizing my teaching skill?

If I have a child who can't hold his hands and legs still and those hands and legs constantly hit his neighbor and I say "I know you're really trying so I have good news and bad news: The good news is no push-ups for you. The bad news is I forgot to bow just now so I'm going to do 25 push-ups." (Therefore we're all doing 25 push-ups!) And as we do them I joke and tease the class about how strong we're getting.

I do push-ups with the class.

Isn't there a chance that, instead of giving them "My way or the highway" ultimatums or worse, ignoring them and through that making them realize their insignificance, keeping those kids in training will potentially create a strong, dynamic, capable, and diverse generation of karateka?

I'm going to slip in two quotes from Albert Einstein here:

"It' is almost a miracle that modern teaching methods have not yet entirely strangled the holy curiosity of inquiry;

for what this delicate little plant needs more than anything, besides stimulation, is freedom.

Everybody is a genius. But if you judge a fish by its ability to climb a tree, it will live its whole life believing that it is stupid."

— Albert Einstein

Sometimes my mind becomes overwhelmed at the thought of what teachers of an internal martial art actually do. Adult students and parents trust us to have the technology and character to judge them, and using that as a basis, help them reinvent themselves as strong, willful, patient warriors.

I'm going to finish with the feedback Sensei Andrew wrote me about the tone of voice post:

*"...in Karate class. I put on some music and then I conduct the entire class in a non-verbal way. I start with exercises, but instead of calling out "50 jumping jacks" I simply start doing jumping jacks in time with the music and everyone follows. To stop an exercise I make a giant [keoske] gesture and then commence with another exercise. Each time I want to start something else I come to [keoske]. My music changes and I change with it moving from exercises to blocking to kata and **I never say a word**.*

The first time I did this I discovered something very interesting. At our 6pm class for the youngest kids I didn't have to say anything at all. At 7pm the next age kids needed only a word or two along the way but in the adult class I needed to speak quite a bit to keep people from just doing whatever they wanted. I attribute this phenomenon to kids being willing to suspend their free will more easily than adults who know everything. The adults didn't instinctively follow like the kids.

I had about 40 minutes of music that played continuously and the class never stopped. At the end I put on some Led Zeppelin and we sparred. The only downside was that after conducting 3 back to back to back classes like this I was physically exhausted, but it was well worth it. Everyone enjoyed it and it's something I plan on doing regularly at our dojo."

Thank YOU Sensei Andrew, for reiterating something I agree exists.....the kids will put themselves completely in our hands and with that comes a great responsibility to teach with care, dignity and grace.

Thanks goes out to ALL people who try to do it.

Kids enjoying a musical workout.

Remaining Passionate as a Teacher
(January 2014)

As a teacher, you and I must continue to reinvent our passion for our chosen art – If we want the student (young and not so young) to take that passion into the next generation, we have to genuinely deliver something that we have done 1000 times, as excitedly as we did the first time. This seems easy, right? Now here's the trick: Even as we're sending our passion genuinely outward, we cannot get caught in the trap of becoming emotionally attached to the daily give and take between ourselves and the material or to the student's reactions to the teaching rituals. To fall into this trap is easy and to remain outside of this self-defeating situation takes vigilance. I'll try to explain.

What brought you to teaching was a love of the subject matter. In the case of teaching fighting techniques, it is easy to love, respect, and even take a bit of selfish ownership. If I am training myself, then it is true, the material is mine – all mine – just like "My Precious" to Gollum. (A reference for Hobbit fans.)

However, if I'm teaching, the minute I teach something it is then about the student and how they fit together with the material, process it, and keep it as THEIR own. This realization got me to thinking about ways teachers let emotions / an administrative fiasco / and opinions change them from passionate and imaginative teachers to guarded and even a little disagreeable.

Here are a couple simple things to remember when trying to avoid this teaching trap:

- When we teach, it is not about us, it is about the student and what they will achieve.
- Most of the time if parents or students are verbally insensitive, it isn't directed at the teacher; it is directed at the frustration due to lack of understanding of the material and the students knee-jerk reaction to remain in the safety of a certain weakness rather than push through to growth.

Many reasons why we do what we do!

- For us to be verbally abusive and insensitive is reactionary and therefore not a sign of a strong spirit. You may remember from blog posts past that I believe that our students are more likely to become what we are, than they are to become what we tell them to become.
- "Every person you deal with is doing the best they can, with what they have to work with, at that moment." This was said to me 20 years ago by a teacher and I remember it to this day. It

explains (but doesn't justify) a lot of conversations.

Here is a much more complicated but effective way to work on this problem:

"My teacher, Master Joe Kelljchian, wrote the Book of Set where he reiterated that we are made up of physicality, chi, brain and emotion."

If we split the emotion: keep emotion going outward – keeping that passion alive, but refuse incoming (by compartmentalizing that skill-set) we give the material passionately but guard against becoming callous due to oversensitivity to administrative chaos, parental impatience, or student confusion.

To remain relevant to my students I constantly have to compartmentalize things like "hurt feelings" when small things happen within my day.

Examples abound: Students show obvious love for another teacher / or their teaching technique, a game I thought would be a great teaching tool flops, the kids are constantly losing focus on my subject but are completely focused on a bug or a car or a person wearing interesting clothes. Then there are the outside distractions: parents who want their child promoted quickly and tell me I'm doing it wrong, administrators who over tax my patience, co-workers who sabotage my class-time. It is self-defeating for me to become emotionally attached to these type events. To remain centered, compartmentalizing my emotion, is to find a way to either incorporate a distraction, re-direct a group, or (as I tell my 5 year old students) just ignore it. If, however, I personalize the emotion and get "mad", I could begin to punish unjustifiably and worse, begin to hold onto events and allow callouses to begin to grow.

So today I'm keeping it short but challenging. If you have more suggestions / tools you've used – please share.

Consistency in Daily Teaching
(July 2014)

As we go back to school, let's remember that even though our lives are bogged down with daily responsibilities, it is important to be unencumbered when we walk into the classroom. (In karate we say "Leave your ego at the door.") How to do it, that is the question.

I've already talked about planning your work, dismissing small annoyances such as administrative details, and projecting passion without letting the passion cause you to take things too personally. So, here is one more hint: Practice projecting consistency.

Be consistent in your love of the material. Be consistent in your classroom management. And please be consistent in who must follow the rules and consistent in what happens when students break the rules.

A few details:

My last post was about retaining your passion in delivering material you've taught hundreds of times before. That can be challenging. The biggest thing I do to seem excited about teaching a basic I've taught many times before is that I actually get excited. Just the other day I was teaching outside blocks to brand new 10 year old kids. It was worth the extra time I took to show the blocks as a self-defense technique. I got excited, and so did they. Even though it was less than 5 minutes of the hour – it was full of spirit that continued into the rest of the class. I didn't notice it at the time. Sitting here now, I picture me doing the blocking system without the excitement – just repeat, repeat and I am sure that these things are true:

- Yelling toward students to create perfection isn't as effective as being part of the quest with them.
- The excitement I bring to a class will be equal to the excitement that students feel, show, and carry with them into their daily lives.
- I am constantly aware of how long I stay on a subject on any given day (It changes with age, as I'm sure yours does. My general rule for children is: The amount of time matches their years on the planet.)
- Tone of voice (May 13, 2010) Karateka have always used voice as a weapon. Consider that when teaching.

Young students and Older students training together can be a challenge

- Remember to individualize expectations for each student.

Classroom Management is interesting because, as teachers, we have a tendency to say "Do what I say, or get out." The problem I have found with that attitude is that I lose students who could really benefit from karate training if only I had a better plan on my classroom (dojo) management. Again, all these years have taught me to have the same rules for everyone. I notice that sometimes teachers have favorites and those favorites get privileges that the other students notice. It is challenging not to overindulge students with talent, while over-chastising students who lack self-control. This makes me ask myself – isn't the quest for self-control one of the things parents put kids in karate to learn? I created a little saying that I use with my kids – *"If one person can do it, then everyone can do it. If everyone cannot do it, than NO ONE can do it."*

This solves small and large issues such as:

- Students who constantly want to tell personal stories during training.
- Students who think they should tell the other students how to improve, rather than wait for the teacher to speak.
- Students who want to quit moving and constantly rest.
- Students who will not hold still. (Notice I didn't say "cannot hold still". That is totally different. That student does exist and should be treated individually…..an exception to the rule.)

The consistency of the "everyone can / no one can" rule is wonderful because everyone understands and it is no longer personal, i.e. "You're really making me mad, Johnny." When I'm managing my students, I'm totally NOT mad, just following the rules of the class. It is easy and most important it is consistent, no matter how tired or distracted I am.

Consistency in who needs to follow the rules is both simple and complicated. Simple because it is everyone, even me! If I drop a weapon, I do push-ups! In my dojo, if we talk about off topic things during training, we do push-ups, and again, if I make a mistake and talk about something off topic – I do the push-ups. It is no big deal!

Students with years of experience have the Responsibility to Teach.

The complication that needs management arises when students who have trained for years have earned the right to be in a leadership position.

Here are two bullets on this subject:

- All the students want to be in that position. This is easy to fix with a short conversation saying "You'll get there, have patience!"
- Some students don't like to follow another student. This takes the support of the teacher toward the student-teacher. I use a quiet voice in the ear of the student that needs reminders. It is quick and efficient.

So it turns out the "technology" (be it karate, math or reading) isn't the hardest part. What makes teaching difficult is constantly reminding myself to have a passionate delivery of the technology, consistent rules that apply to everyone, not just the kids that may be labeled as hard to handle, and a calm delivery of those rules. I laugh when I reread how easy it sounds and remember how difficult it is minute by minute, day after day. By now, you know I like feedback, so let me know your thoughts.

CHAPTER 3
VARIETY OF WORKOUTS

Let's Mix Up the Repetition
(June 2009)

Try These Changes to Start Your Class:
1. Playing Sensei Says
2. Taking numbers up and numbers down (ex: 10 jumping jacks, 20 pushups, 30 mountain climbers...then when you get to a certain number start going down; ex: 40 front kicks, 30 toe touches, 20 front punches.)
3. Turn a certain word into a "key" word: ex: Karate would mean 5, jumping jacks, 5 pushups, and 5 mountain climbers, and Rules would mean 5 sit ups, 5 leg lifts and 5 calf raises. Do basics and stretches. Every few minutes yell out one or both of the words to get the exercises in.
4. Use a medicine ball game in between each exercise.
   Try one or all four and let me know how it works out.

I need to digress into the word osu for a moment. I love the word, and I love it's meaning of "I understand, let's push on." Here is my dilemma: although I know the proper spelling of the word is "osu", I love the word spelled oos. I came to karate spelling the word oos, and for sentimental, nostalgic reasons, will continue to spell it that way when I use it in future posts. I hope this isn't a deal breaker for you, and that my quirkiness will not turn you off to the information here.

Now let's get down to the business of separating the children into classifications for future. When I teach children age 3 to 5+ I call it "pre-karate". You can see a few in this photo.

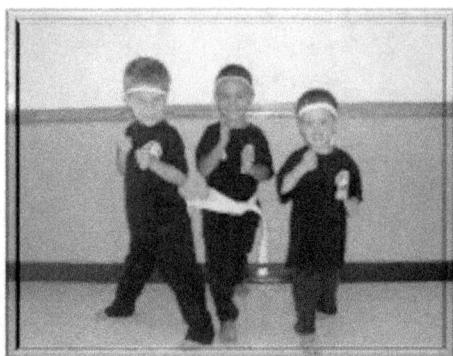

This group does not get rank, is non-competitive, does not have to bow at the dojo door, learn Japanese, and does not do push-ups for punishment. I'd like to mention why I don't have my 'babies' do push-ups for punishment: My goal with these youngsters is to make them LOVE exercise. Therefore, using push-ups as punishment is contrary to my goal. It seems pretty logical to me. What do you think? You can get a clear understanding of my view on these little guys from my book, *Kicks with Kids, Martial Arts for the Very Young*.

Age 6 to 12+ - Begins the pathway to serious training. I call these children mainstream because they are easily capable of understanding the rules and etiquette in the dojo and they are completely capable of being competitive and reaching goals, both personal and rank oriented.

Here is a photo with a few kids who have just begun this journey:

Age 10 to 13+ with the rank of 3rd Kyu or higher is a tough group to teach. These children have been training for anywhere from 4 to 8 years. They are not qualified to test for black belts yet and are no longer interested in the same training games the little children experience.

At some point they will join the adult class and begin rigorously preparing for their black belt test. However, for a few years between reaching brown belt (in my Japanese system) and being mature enough to want to be in the adult class, they require some interesting teaching tactics. I won't spoil them. Yet, it is important that I treat them like young adults and keep them knowledgeable of everything that karate has to offer them. I have found this to be challenging. I will detail more on this in a future post. Write me if you have any specific ideas you would like to see in that post.

I have had a significant number of special needs children travel through my dojo. (I bet you have too!) I keep them with the mainstream group and we find very little adjustments need to be made for everyone to be comfortable. Have you had the same experience?

That does segue me to an axiom I teach my assistant instructors:

In a children's class, children come first, and technology is second. In an adult class you reverse that.

A brief explanation:

My goal with the kids is to make them feel stronger, more capable, and more empowered when they leave class than when they arrived

If, in order to achieve that, I have to let a stance correction slide till another lesson, no problem. In reverse, the adult training is all about the technology. We work and improve from the beginning to the end of every lesson. "Feeling better" about yourself (I smile when I type that, it is so silly), is the responsibility of the adult practitioner – not the responsibility of me, the instructor.

Sparring
(September 2009)

Oos, Thanks to those who have been writing me. Ironically, I got the most feedback from the post on the games (drills). It turns out that many of you knew about spin and find the knife, but had forgotten it existed. According to your feedback, the kids are psyched that it is back!

Now… we push on……..

The three big pillars on which training is based are kata, sparring, and self-defense.

My last post on kata gave you one workout to keep the kata repetition interesting. There are many other ways to change up the kata repetition. In future posts I will brainstorm some. In the meantime, write me with your ideas.

Today let's begin to talk about sparring. The first thing I'd like to do is list the ways children grow from sparring. Sparring teaches us to:

- *Keep our hands up*
- *Block, punch, kick, and move around all at the same time. (Keep both an offensive and a defensive mentality running simultaneously.)*
- *Stay calm and allow for spontaneity in the midst of chaos.*
- *Learn techniques and set strategies.*
- *Aim.*
- *And finally, sparring gives us a superior aerobic workout*

Next, let's review the place of light contact and hard contact in sparring. When I was a kyu, Master Kelljchian used the terms 'Go *kumite*' and '*Ju kumite*' to describe what he wanted us to do on any given day. All competitions that I have been attending in recent years have encouraged *Ju kumite* with the children.

I have been playing with the difference in hard contact, and soft contact with my children's classes for years. Here is the compromise that has been working best for me.

When the children are sparring the teachers, it is a good time to practice their hard contact. When they are sparring each other, they need to use control.

The biggest obstacle in getting them to use control is that children think that they must hit slower in order to hit with control. (And conversely, when they go fast they lose everything BUT power. They often forget to aim, or plan their technique.)

In order to work on controlled hitting, I tell the kids to imagine the opponent is on fire and when you touch them pull away like you're getting burnt. It is a slow and tedious learning curve, but we all get there.

WARNING - Anecdotal Story: I remember being a kyu and watching as Master Kelljchian had an adult student try to use focus on a concrete wall to try to teach the adult student to pull his punches. I don't use that method with kids, but it proves that Ju kumite has been around a very long time and has a place in training.

How and when do I let the children begin to do harder contact on each other?

I like to wait until the children are 10ish, or brown belts, or both. Then, the first step for me is to gear them up with chest pads and head gear with face masks. By putting the extra padding on them, I remove some of the fear of getting hit. Since the children have had practice hitting us hard, they don't really have trouble hitting hard. Very few people like getting hit hard when they first experience it. It takes getting used to. Hence, the added gear. I encourage face masks for most of their teen life because broken noses, and black eyes are unacceptable to me for children and teens.

Once the teens move up to the adult class, they become more focused, serious, and willing to take risks. (I encourage this transition at around age 12 and expect it at age 13, but have had a few exceptions in all directions over the years.) Adult training makes practitioners more aware of their power, the use of technique and setting up techniques with a strategy. At this point the facemasks, and added chest protection probably aren't necessary.

This shot shows Kyle (age 11) and Cody (around 16) sparring in adult class.

All of us spar the kids, and have the kids spar each other. I always put gloves and heads on kids sparring other kids. Sparring without gear allows too much chance for injury.

Here are a few variations on sparring for kids:
-2 on 1-

Description:

This is a standard drill in the adult class. When I do it with kids, I make the adults the "1" and two kids go against him / her. Expect chaos and a lot of laughter.

Details of Interest:

When the kids are advanced, I'll let them take the role of the "1", but I still keep an adult in the mix – to keep things under control. I also keep these matches 30 to 45 seconds, for safety.

-Team sparring-

Description:

Depending on the amount of kids in class, I create teams consisting of 4 – 6 kids. I start with a brown or purple belt captain. Then I choose from the green belts and put an equal amount on each team. Then I do the same with the three stripers, the two stripers, and the beginners. I like to keep the talent split evenly within all the teams. (Occasionally I have uneven numbers, but that is easy to fix. Just let one team member spar twice.) I set the matches at 30 – 45 seconds. Each team is encouraged to come up with a name. (Some of the names I have heard over the years.......Yikes!) Then I let the kids send in one fighter and the other team tries to send in a match. Sparring continues and we add up the team score. My favorite ending is when we get to the end of the last match and the score is tied. Next point wins. I get to explain that the outcome is going to be what it is going to be. However, both teams sparred well. That is how the score got so close.

After we determine the winning team, I give the losing team donkey kicks. Then I turn around and give the winning team 5 more donkey kicks than the losing team. (Usually 10 and 15)

My reasoning here is two-fold: First, I want them to remember that I am unpredictable, and will do things that don't make sense to them. And secondly, the backwards reward makes everyone talk more about how weird I am than about who won and lost. I love to get my kids to think about the adventure more than the outcome.

Details of Interest:

An additional benefit to running this game is that I can use this venue to teach my adult kyus to judge and keep score, and I can teach my new black belts to center rings!

This game (drill) builds camaraderie among the students, and gives them a chance to practice their sportsmanship (karate courtesy) when there is nothing at stake. This game takes almost an entire class – about 45 minutes. One more thing: You can do this game with kata as well!

The "One Step" Game

Description: Place each child around the room with about 3 feet of space around them. (In large classes, I have to divide the class into two groups to play this game.) Then explain how to play:

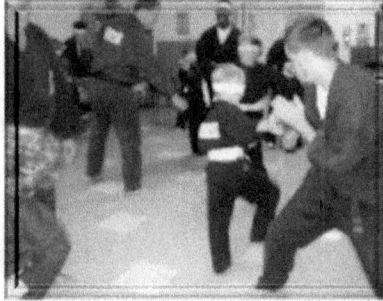

The children will remain in their spots. We adults will walk around and touch or grab their arms, shoulders, and tops of their heads.

When they feel us there, and taking ONLY one step in any direction, the child will try to hit, kick, or escape. They should use lots of *kiais*. The trick is that the child will pull their headband over their eyes. They won't be able to see us. For safety, explain that if ANY adult voice yells "*yame* / stop", everyone in the room should freeze because one child could be about to hit another child and we need a minute to reset the spacing. Then play!

Details of Interest:

This game doesn't require sparring gear. Also, I am a strict teacher where cheating is concerned. I explain to the kids NOT to try to peak, but instead enjoy the adventure knowing they are safe with us. If they continue to try to cheat, I have them sit down and watch the rest of the game. I try to be very consistent in my expectations where courtesy, honesty, and character are concerned. Please keep making our kids into strong *karateka*.

Five Drills for Variety in Training
(July 2009)

I hope that some of the hints that I've mentioned have come in handy and that you and your students are having an adventurous time in the dojo.

I am going to make a list of drills (I call them games) you can put into different portions of the training. Try one or all of them and let me know how they work for you. Some of these drills were used when I was a kyu, in an adult class. I will mark those with an asterisk.

Shark and Eagle*

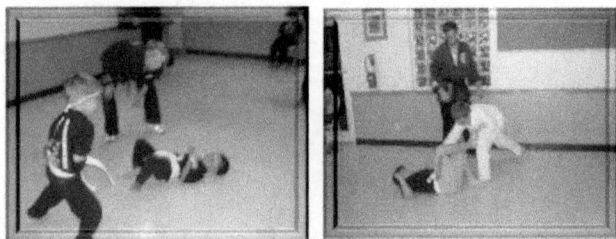

Description of Drill: Place one student in a ground fighting position and one in a fighting stance. Have the standing student try to tag the ground fighting student with a kick or a punch in the belly or the head. Have the ground fighting student use his guard position, movement on the ground, and kicking / grabbing to defend.

When to use it: This one works at the beginning, middle, and end of class. There is no end to the uses of this game.

Other details of interest: Everyone loves this game, even adults. This drill really improves the student's ability to move in the ground fighting position and the attack from the ground.

Spin and Find the Knife

Description of Drill:

Get a rubber knife. (This also works with a wooden gun and even karate weapons.) Have all the kids stand in a circle and explain how to play: One child will go into the middle of the circle and start spinning around "helicopter" style.

While he is spinning, you drop the knife somewhere in the circle. After he is sufficiently dizzy, have him stop and try to find the knife, pick it up by the handle, and take his guard position. Let everyone have a turn.

When to use it:

Good at the end of the day, or after working knife techniques. It really opens the door for discussion on the danger of weapons.

Other details of interest: This is a popular game. As an adult kyu, we played this game to simulate what it feels like to have your ears boxed. That came in handy later when I did have my ears boxed. What a case of vertigo!!

Blocker

Description of Drill: The blocker is a staple when teaching blocking systems to anyone under the age of 8. After the repetition of the blocking system, use the blocker to hit the children. I hit them, first in the order that I worked the blocks and then randomly, strictly for the laughter. All ages like it, but under the age of 8 it is the 'reward' for staying focused.

When to use it: Obviously, this drill fits best after working repetition on blocking, whether at the beginning, middle, or end of class.

Other details of interest: Although the blocker wasn't around when I was a kyu, it is a daily tool in my teaching bag. I try to bring it to every class and miss it when I forget. Even though this photo shows one student and teacher. More often, I am using a blocker on 10 or more kids at the same time. I am running up and down the rows and they are blocking and laughing. Everyone is getting stronger.

Blocker vs. Blocker

Description of Drill:

Hand each child a blocker and let them strike at each other. Before you let them start, explain that the soft part of the blocker is the hitting part. If they hit with the handle it will hurt them both. (Inevitably, someone will catch their finger in the clashing handles, but at least you warned them.)

When to use it: This game fits in the middle and at the end of class. It is a great stress reliever if you have been focusing on technology for a long period. Or, it is a treat instead of sparring at the end of class.

Other details of interest: The kids call this playing "star wars". Try it once and watch their excitement. Let me know if your kids love it as much as mine.

Double-Ended Blockers

Description of Drill:

Each participant has a double ended blocker and they block and strike each other for an allotted period of time. I keep my matches under 45 seconds to keep the injuries down.

When to use it: It is an end of the day game. I use it about 4 times a year as a special event.

Other details of interest: In this picture, Cody and Kyle are having some fun, don't you think? This game requires 4 blockers and 2 couplers. This is about a $50 or $75 investment. (I have tried making my own out of PVC and padding, but they don't hold up, they are too heavy, and they don't work very well.

Jump rope

Description of Drill:

The jump rope I am referring to is about 10 feet long. Hook one end to a chair and hold the other end. Have the participants earn their jump rope turn by answering a karate question or showing a karate skill. I give them three choices of how to pass through the rope:

1. Just run through the turning rope.
2. Just jump rope and run out when you have jumped 5 or more times. (That is up to the teacher. Make sure everyone is allowed to jump the same number of times).
3. Run in and jump rope (5 times). Run out when you are done.

When to use it: This game fits in all parts of training. I use it almost exclusively at the end of class. I use the game to review history and philosophy of karate by having the students answer in order to get their turn.

Other details of interest:

This drill is as popular as any of the drills I use. It is, as all my drills are, a way to vary the repetition of training. It also builds timing, speed, and agility in movement. The first time I ever saw anyone using the jump rope was while teaching with Sensei Nick Brown over 20 years ago. I have tweaked it a little over the years, but have been using consistently throughout my teaching.

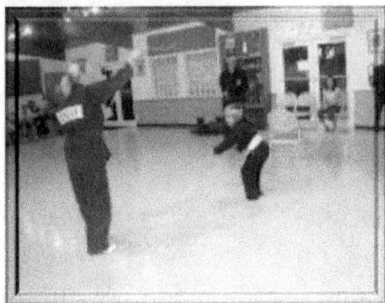

One quick note: If your class is oversized (30 kids) it might take 25 or 30 minutes to do some of these drills. Therefore, I recommend that you divide the children into groups of 10. One group can work stretch, exercise, basics etc. One group can work technology. One group can "play" with one of these drills. If you try to do 30 children in the jump rope game or the spin and find the knife game or the blocker vs. blocker game, the kids have too much down time and it isn't good use of the time.

Use the drills and let me know if you have questions, failures, or successes.

Self Defense and Kids
(October & November 2009)

Here's one idea I would like to propose:

Go into your dojo and create a game where you test the reactions of your kids (age 6 - 10, rank 9th - 5th kyu) to grabs and punches. See what is consistent, and what is forgotten.

Please remember that the children change drastically between the ages of 5 and 13. Most of our new students are between the ages of 5 and 8. Once they are older, and / or more experienced, their learning curve will reflect that. Now, on to the self-defense:

When children are young, and new to training, learning their self defense can be confusing.

All of us, as black belts, have favorite follow up techniques. Who doesn't love a well-placed empi or a timely used earclap!

It has been my experience that too many choices in follow up strikes can cause confusion, and lack of spontaneity in new, young *karateka*.

I have had really good results by using the same follow up strike series with all their techniques. It sounds boring to us, because we thrive with many options. However, too many options with young, new white belts is an invitation to confusion. Students age 5 to 10ish, rank 9th kyu to 7th kyu (the first year of training) could build a strong defensive plan based on a few follow up ideas.

The strikes I use are the shotei and a heel stomp.

However, there are many simple combinations you could use. If you are not already incorporating this idea, try this experiment:

Go into your dojo and do some self-defense with your beginners. Then do a "game" of reactionary drills at the end of class. Pay specific attention to the follow up strikes. If the strikes are slow to come, or tentative, try teaching the same strikes on EVERY grab for the next month. Then play the "game" again. Hopefully, you will see a difference in the young, novice's ability to retain this important information.

Two of my favorite ways to practice (and observe) what self-defense has been memorized are reactionaries and *bunkai*.

Reactionaries

This is simple. Place all the children in a circle. Using yourself and your helpers walk from person to person and do all the grabs you are teaching (front extended, rear extended, wrists, bearhugs, and the punch). Don't tell the kids which one you are going to do, of course. See which children remember what. I like to encourage children to run after they hit back (follow-up). This will be a necessary addition in the event of a real danger.

Bunkai

We all know what *bunkai* is. However, where kids building bunkai with kids is concerned there are a few pointers that might come in handy. Keep it simple. Let them do the inventing. Let them have fun.

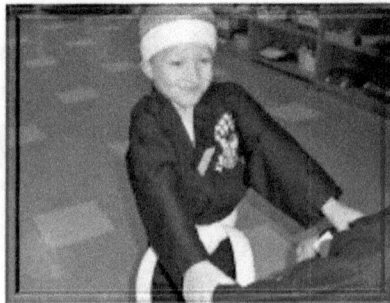

Don't think too much about how it reflects on you. If it seems silly to you, it is probably pretty cool to them. I would like to remind you to teach your children two of the old traditional ideas regarding *bunkai*.

The first one is: whoever starts the fight loses. We all know this. It is a basic in karate because karate is defensive. The second tradition is that the higher ranking person is the defender / winner. Once the kids understand that rank traditionally wins, I break the rule often. I do, however, think it is important to pass those traditions on to the next generation.

Now I'd like to digress in two directions. *First, I would like to talk about the younger child.*
Have you ever had a problem making the child understand if he (she) was the *uke* (bad guy) or the defender (good guy)? I call self-defense good guy / bad guy for the first year of training. I have noticed a specific pattern where children age 5 and 6 have trouble understanding which role they are in and what to do in that role. One trick I have used is to "mark" the bad guy (*uke*) with a piece of tape.

Then the beginning child knows that when he is wearing the tape, he is the bad guy (*uke*) and he doesn't do the follow-up strikes. This has cut down on chaos. Another area that I have modified for my younger kids is aim and follow through. It is my opinion, that when kids are very young, they don't know (nor maybe should they) how to pull or control their strikes to the face. To that end, when I am having the children aim shotei strikes, I have them aim beside the face and use complete extension of the arm. I tell them this: "Fake bad guy, fake face; Real bad guy, real face." Has your experience in children's self-defense been very different?

Now I would like to spend a minute on older children.

These kids have been training a year plus and are 6th kyu or higher. The first thing I'd like to cover is that it is definitely time to add variations to the follow ups. I have done this with older children (9 – 12) that are still quite young in rank with good results. I like to have the basic follow-up strike pattern memorized as a back-up. However, older children like everything from ear-claps to elbow strikes, to groin strikes. They get psyched at the idea of defending themselves.

With the 6th kyu and older, I have also had good results when I began adding new techniques. An example of this is in the wrist grab. My standard technique for a wrist grab is "point upward" with a heel stomp, palm heel follow up. The next addition, when the child is ready is two-fold.

1. I explain how the point technique works, move the thumb placement as the uke (bad guy) and begin the road to understanding technique. The photo shows a reverse wrist grab.

2. I start to work some standard adult information. Examples include a traditional Goju technique called tiger neck takedown (a child favorite) and an old straight punch technique where the follow-up is four elbow strikes.

3. All the while, with kids of all ages, like you, I'm working traditional mat work: break falls and rolls. This will prepare them for the falling that is involved in the harder techniques and the wrestling that is to come.

Here are some important reminders on self defense:

- When children are new to karate and under the age of 12, it might help NOT to allow too many choices in their follow-up strikes. Keep it simple and build confidence for the first year.
- The two "games" that test how they are doing are one where you are the attacker and they must react without previous knowledge of which attack is coming and *bunkai*.
- Continue to do basic mat work, of course.
- Just like the kata become more difficult with time, the self-defense becomes more intricate as the rank and age increase. This intricacy is two-fold: more techniques and more variation on each technique.

More Karate Games for Fun and Learning
(February 2012)

I was talking to one of my kid's classes about the activities (games, exercises, drills – pick your favorite word here) that I run at the end of class. We had an impromptu vote on which activity was anyone's favorite.

Here are some (in no particular order), according to my Friday afternoon class:

Sparring

Description of Drill:

Everyone knows sparring, I am sure. So I will quickly mention one thing. To me, the most difficult part of sparring at the children's level is teaching them to hit adults hard but use control when they are with one another. What do you think?

When to Use it:

Sparring is versatile. It fits in all parts of class; beginning, middle, and end. Sometimes I start a children's class with sparring. Then I'll run exercises at the end of class. (When I do, I play a crazy game for the exercises portion. I will discuss that in another post.)

I'm sure all of you have spent the entire class sparring. Sixty minutes of sparring works great with older kids, but isn't as good if the kids are young and have a short attention span. Traditionally, sparring comes in the last 1/3 of class.

Other Details of Interest:

Too many details, too little time. So, here is a tidbit of interest: Do you remember that in the book The Karate Dojo, Peter Urban mentions that someone who is a good fighter is generally not great at kata and vice versa? What do you think about that? I definitely try to raise students who value and perform both equally. It is a challenge.

Throwing Weapons

Description of Drill:

This one is easy. We already do it in every weapons seminar. All weapons can be thrown. I choose which weapons to throw and what throwing game to use based on the age and rank of the children. Young children (5 ish) do best with *escrimas*. One step older, and more experienced and I can add *bo*. Add another year or two to the children's age and I can move on to *sai* etc.

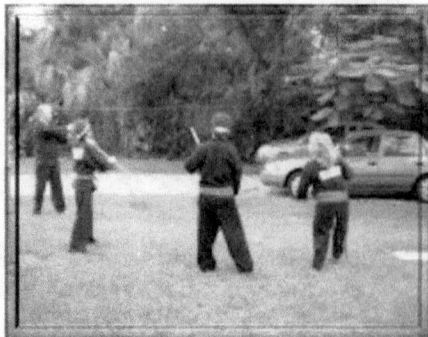

We all know that weapons can be thrown at an object and to a partner. Both games are popular in my dojo. As a change, I will sometimes let the kids throw bos and escrimas as far as they can, just for the fun of distance.

When to Use it: This is an end of the day game for sure. I usually use it at the end of a day where one of two things has been going on. 1. I'll use this game when we have been working weapons. 2. This game also works at the end of a day when we have been focused all hour on a difficult, detailed concept and everyone is worn out. This game doesn't take long (10 minutes?) and it is exciting for kids. (After all it made the top 7, out of about 20 different choices!)

Other Details of Interest:

This will be the first time that some of the children have been near a target event (throwing at an object). It will definitely be the first time they have been allowed to throw weapons to another person. This is a perfect opportunity to emphasize safety, courtesy and self-control in students. I like to address these aspects before the event. That way, if the students lack one of these important characteristics, they are aware of what I expect. Therefore, the conversation, and punishment, that follows will not be a surprise. A few important things you might mention include these: When throwing and catching make sure you throw TO the partner and not AT him. When throwing at a target make sure everyone who isn't throwing waits behind the throwing line.

Through the Wall

Description of Drill: This is a variation on Red Rover. This is how I play it: All my adult helpers and I make a "wall". These kids break through the wall one at a time. They should use their wit, power, kiai, and any strikes they want and can remember. (I tell my adults to cover their teeth and their groin.)

It is exciting and adventurous for the kids and it builds fighting spirit. A little craziness is a perfect way to end a day.

When to Use it:

This is an end of the day game. It takes quite a bit of time (about 1 minute per child). So you have to allow enough time to give everyone a turn.

Other Details of Interest: This game builds confidence and releases power without restriction. It is loud, fun and a little unpredictable. As the children grow older (11+) they will begin to transition from wanting to break through the wall, to wanting to become part of the wall. This is one of the signs that they are ready to move into the adult class.

Dark Game

Description of Drill:

Insanity rules in this variation of a haunted house. Basically, my helpers and I turn out all the lights and invite the children one at a time to come in one door and get out the other. We incorporate the blockers, punching bags, noodles and some basic grabs into the obstacles that the kids need to maneuver as they make their way from the front door to the back. We also take into account the children's age and rank when we decide how difficult and scary to make the adventure.

This photo shows what it looks like to the kids - Very Dark.

When to Use it:

The last game of class is the best place to put the dark game. Like break through the wall, this drill is time consuming. I like to allow a few minutes after the game to talk about it. Everyone will want to mention their personal experience. Then I mention how weird it is when it is too dark to see what is going on.

Other Details of Interest: This is a variation on a drill Master Kelljchian used to run with us. The drill then was done at night, outside, and usually accompanied a lot of injuries. I keep it a little safer for my kids.

Bunkai

Description of Drill:

We all know what bunkai is. (Please excuse any spelling variation that you disagree with.) A quick definition would be that basically, we choreograph a fight for the kids. At the end of the class, everyone performs their bunkai (with proper bows, of course). This activity is a big hit with our parent audience. *When to use it:* I usually put bunkai at the end of a day when I have emphasized self-defense techniques. Obviously, I use the techniques I taught that night in the bunkai. This gives the kids a chance to do the techniques spontaneously, thereby learning that things rarely go as planned!

Other details of interest:

Bunkai builds many skills that I want in my students. It is creative, builds independence, and reinforces the memory of self-defense technique. This also builds leadership skills in the highest ranking person in the group (which is not necessarily the most outgoing person in the group). For variety, and as the kids get older and more experienced, try incorporating weapons into the bunkai.

One more note: I try to do sparring every third class. That allows me two classes to do another game (activity) with the kids. There are a few reasons why I do this. I have found that if I do sparring every week, it becomes too common and the kids take it for granted: thinking of it as wasted time, or play time. Also, there are many aspects of training that can be strengthened from another game. A few of these aspects include: agility, power, coordination, creativity, and even courage. Finally, I have found that when kids shy away from sparring, they often rise to the idea of blocker v.s. blocker or the dark game. There is something for everyone if I use all the activities available.

A Weapons Class for Variety and Fun
(April 2010)

I would like to talk about weapons. Most of our Goju syles do weapons in some form. For example, USAGF has weapons seminars that the children can challenge themselves by attending. I have found that another way weapons can be used to the benefit of the student and teacher is by including them (especially escrima and bo) as a tool to change the stretch and exercise routine. Using weapons at the beginning of class is a great way to introduce kids to the responsibility needed to handle something that is potentially dangerous. It is also a great way to get around the boredom of repetitive exercising. And, another benefit is that touching the weapons often builds hand eye coordination. I will talk about two different plans that can incorporate weapons into the children's routine.

Plan 1: There are only two of us teaching. One of us runs an entire class based on weapons, while the other person takes out individuals or small groups for their kata / rank technology work.

Plan 2: If I have enough helpers, I can spend the first third of the class stretching, exercising and doing basics with the weapons. The middle of the class is used for rank oriented kata and technology. I use all my helpers and we divide the kids into small groups. Each of us does what we can to impart a little more technology to each child. Finally, at the end of the day we will either throw the weapon or build a simple weapons bunkai. I decide which "game" based on the amount of time left in the class.

Having said that, here is a sample class:

Let's start by saying that I am assuming that one person will be running weapons for 50 (out of 60) minutes. Another teacher will be pulling small groups for Rank based work in 7 to 10 minute increments. (Plan 1.)

Here is a suggestion on what to do:

You will need enough escrima sticks for all the students. Spend the first 2 – 3 minutes explaining that this is a real karate weapon. Not a toy. The escrima stick really hurts people. Therefore, it cannot be played with at all. No swinging, flipping, twirling, or throwing without permission from Sensei. This is how I want you to stand while I explain what we're going to do next.... And show them how to stand in keoske.

Even though I am including a fairly detailed workout, don't limit yourself to my choices. Use the lists below as suggestions.

Start with stretching, exercising, and dexterity. (about 10 minutes) When I do this part of class, I don't lump all the exercises together. I do a stretch, an exercise, and a dexterity. Then I repeat that. The children in this workout situation are not required to understand which one is the exercise, and which is the dexterity. So, let them have more variety and fun!

Here are some suggestions:

Stretches:

Seated pike, Bend side to side, Twist right & left, Stretch the shoulders, Seated straddle, Butterfly

Exercises: Jumping jacks, Push ups, Mountain climbers, Leg lifts, Running in place, Sit ups

Dexterity: Throw from hand to hand, Finger twirls, Alternate catches, Pass behind back, Balance on one finger and catch, 180 degree throws

Now show a fighting position, some blocks and some strikes. (15 minutes)

Here are some suggestions:

Weapon vs Empty Hand:
1. Do a simple escape from a front choke (hands on the shoulders of the opponent). Follow up with a kick.

2. Do a simple escape from a front choke (hands on the shoulders of the opponent). Follow up with a U punch using the weapon.
3. Do an escape from a rear bear hug. Follow up with a back kick.
4. Do an escape from a rear bear hug. Follow up with a poke to the ribs of the attacker.

Weapons vs Weapon:

1. From Fighting Position: Use the weapon to block an overhead attack. Follow up with a U punch with the weapon.
2. From Fighting Position: Use the weapon to a strike coming from the side. Follow up with a poke with the weapon.
3. From a Fighting Position: Use the weapon to block an overhead attack. Follow up with a front kick.
4. From a Fighting Position: Use the weapon to block a strike coming from the side. Follow up with a side kick.

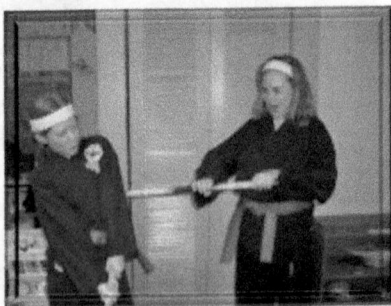

5. Teach the group how to block over, under, and side to side. Then teach the

group how to hit over under, side to side. Let them try blocking and striking for 4 strikes. Keep an eye on the kids while they are doing this. It is a little dangerous, but fun.

Don't forget that your helper has been pulling small groups for their rank technology throughout all this weapons work. Each group has missed some part of your work. However, it is my experience that the kids have enough time with me to be ready to push on. At this point we are somewhere between ½ and 2/3rds of the way through class. This is where you must assess what else you can get done.

In order to do this you will want to answer these few questions: Did helpers show up? Do you have more or less than a dozen kids in the room? Have you got some higher ranking kids that can lead and essentially help you?

Depending on the answers to the questions, pick between:

    a) Taking the kids outside and letting them throw the weapons, or

b) Dividing them into small enough groups that they can build little bunkai based on the technique you were teaching. If you have helpers and ½ the class left, you can build the bunkai and watch all the skits. It is pretty cool.

If you don't have time to build bunkai, the kids will really love throwing.

At the end of class, you will have a great opportunity to teach the group about the courtesy involved in bowing with weapons.

They can sit in their formal kneeling position, show respect to the weapon, meditate, and bow.... All with the weapon.

If you want to apply the above workout in "Plan 2" the adjustment is easy.

Shorten the times to allow a technology station in the middle of class. It will go something like this:

- 10 minutes to introduce the weapon, and do stretch etc.

- 7 or 8 minutes for the striking drills.
- 10 minutes of technology work.
- 10 minutes to build bunkai, 10 minutes to watch it and 5 minutes to bow out.

If you want to throw the weapon instead of building bunkai, you can add time to all the other stations.I hope you all find success with this workout. Keep me posted on how you are doing.

Sparring Games
(December 2010)

Recently, I tried two training games (drills?) that I hadn't used before. The kids and my assistant teachers liked them both.

1. I'll call this one "Good Sport, Bad Sport". Start by pairing two kids together in a typical, point match. Explain in the beginning of the match that the plan is to be a good sport whether you win or lose. Keep score. Then the winner and the loser both practice good sportsmanship. (I call good sportsmanship karate courtesy.) Do the match again, and this time practice bad sportsmanship and that is even more fun. There is whining and pouting and gloating. It is loud and riotous.

2. The next game starts by putting the kids in a very large circle facing inward. The adults are in a circle within the circle and they are facing outward. Start playing music and everyone starts scooting in the circle, keeping their hands up and finding their rhythm. (In my experiment, the kids went clockwise and the adults went counter-clockwise.) When the music stops, if the child is in front of an adult, he (or she) attempts to score a point. Children who don't have an adult in front of them, shadow box (work their technique on an imaginary opponent). This drill continues for some minutes and in the process everyone gets excited. Everyone gets to practice being quick off the line. This game was popular with all the participants. I will definitely do it again.

Safety Day
(June 2011)

It is nice to have time to sit and think about teaching. On the subject of street-wise safety and children, I'm certain we all have methods that have been working for us for years. I hope to get a lot of feedback on this. Thanks for telling me what is working in your dojos. I'm not sure how long I've been running a "Safety Day". I know I began doing it at summer camps and moved it into my dojo to change the routine a little. It worked so well, that I have kept it up for years. I have a flyer I give out when I teach safety and I'm going to include it below:

As you can read, the information is basic, but pertinent to a safe lifestyle.

Here is how I breakdown the hour long workout:

TALK ABOUT SAFETY

First, I divide the kids into age groups (Don't forget I am blessed with assistant teachers. I will address what I do when I am alone a little later):

>age 5 & 6
>
>age 7 through 8 or 9
>
>age 10 and 11
>
>age 12 and up (if they are still training as children)

Each group gets a teacher and each group starts by looking over the sheet. We talk about the importance of knowing what city you live in, how to dial 911, and other common sense details. When we get to the "ALWAYS" category, I let people play What if this happens?

When we get to the "NEVER" category, I play a game where we pretend we're walking on the wrong side of the road. A car pulls up opens the passenger door, and tries to pull our arm to get us in the car and speed away. Then we repeat the game while walking FACING traffic and note the safety difference.

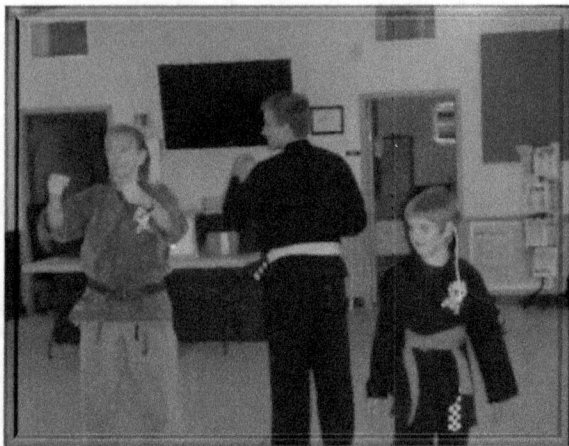

A quick note: the reason I divide the children by age is based on how to address the different age groups. I will speak to a preteen clearly and honestly. When speaking to a 5 year old, who is always with a parent, the parameters are completely different.

When we talk about being home alone, and being outside alone, we also play 'what if' games and move a little. After all, sitting and talking can get pretty boring. Of course, I play an attacker and the kids can kick, hit and "YELL, YELL, YELL. That is the best part so far!

All the kids take a sheet home so they can talk about everything with their parents. (I also include a safety day flyer in my introduction packets.)

Heel stomps, Palm Heel strikes Elbows and Knees are all examples of follow up strikes I use

BAG WORK

All ages move into bag work. All the students hit, kick and scream.

TECHNIQUES

We work techniques on a regular basis, so most of this is review. When working self defense, I try to structure the technique to the age and power of my students. Young students use simple follow up strikes that are realistic against a larger assailant. Older children have more power, better memory, and a stronger opinion of what they want as far as follow up (i.e. how to hit back). Each group works at their own level.

This is a great place for me to mention that the target area in sparring is belly and head, but the target area in daily self defense is groin, knees, nose, throat, the areas that really hurt people. Many children (and adults) take a long time to make that distinction!

USING DAILY ITEMS IN SELF DEFENSE aka THE MOST FUN PART OF THE CLASS

The last activity of the workout is another "what if". What if you are standing, waiting for the bus (or a movie, or a friend) and a stranger approaches? It is a simple game meant to encourage the children to throw an object that they are holding at potentially dangerous individuals. Punching bags play the part of back packs, purses, lunchboxes and video games. My helpers and I play the dangerous individuals. We storm in on them and they throw things scream and run for help. It is chaotic, energy building and fun; a perfect period at the end of the safety day sentence.

WHEN I TEACH ALONE

If I am teaching alone, I keep the order of events the same. When talking about routines indoors and out I simply add the idea that what is correct when you're 6 isn't the same at age 10. We talk about it together. In the area of bag work, technique, and throwing things I let the older children help me with the younger ones. Then, at the end of each station, the older kids show their power and skill on me. Tell me about your routines.

CHAPTER 4
One More Thing

Kids and Competition
(November 2010)

"Character is what you have left when you've lost everything you can lose." Evan Esar

That is a great quote. Karate teachers are in the business (art form) of creating character. Most of us have had days when we questioned whether to stay in training, when we had to pull ourselves up by our boot straps and try again. If we stayed in training, that thing that didn't kill us DID make us stronger....lesson learned.

Competition is one of the experiences that builds character.

We've all been there and we all know the strength of character that can emerge from the experience. Competition makes the students practice, causes them to deal with nervousness, and allows them to see their peer group in action. Having said that, here are 3 bullets that I would like to challenge you to think about:

- *How young is too young?*
- *Are there certain types of children where competition might be harmful?*

- *What is the responsibility of the center judge to be clear, non-biased, and welcoming in the ring? How does the conversation to and about the competitors from the judges affect the competitors self- view?*

Let's Talk About Age

In my opinion children younger than 6 are too young to compare themselves to other children. (There is an exception here and there in life. I know that.) For the most part, since really young children are just realizing that they are not the center of the universe, and that other children might be faster, funnier, smarter….it might set a downward spiral to exaggerate the width of that gap by having them constantly go to competitions and lose.

For my very young students I create a demonstration situation and give everyone the same prize. If they stay long enough in karate, they will have plenty of time to experience competition. Talk to your little ones and more importantly HEAR that they don't really realize that they are going to be compared. Before you test their mettle, give your very young students a chance to create a strong self-image through encouragement and humor.

Exceptional Students

"Karate is for everyone, but everyone is not for karate." Do you remember that old saying? Here is another one: "Who is the one person that you cannot teach? The student who doesn't want it." The point of those two sayings is that we get all kinds of kids. We get children with obvious learning challenges. When sending our special needs children, we know to talk to the people running the event, so they can be sure to create a positive experience.

However, we also get children with less obvious learning challenges like ADHD (saying they can't sit still is an understatement), and Asperger's (exaggerated attention disorder, with compulsive tendencies).My rule of thumb, when centering a ring, is to assume that a child is not being intentionally disrespectful and not bark my commands. That way, if the children have special circumstances, no one will be hurt.

There is another situation that is less visible. What about a child who doesn't have a label, loves the training, loves to fight, but doesn't have a great confidence line in life or in showmanship? I know that we all realize how much this child needs the dojo and how much he shouldn't be pressured into competition. To make matters more complicated, this child is usually quiet, and does what he is told....so his discomfort will go unnoticed until he quits showing up for training. The best case scenario is that the teacher works directly with the parents and everyone watches the growth and development with ease and comfort. If this child ends up in your ring, be gentle in their lack of fighting spirit, or their lack of natural physical talent. They are gaining so much more from their training, don't you think?

The Role of the Center Judge

All of us have stories of judges who made us feel like they knew us, even though they didn't. All of us have had the opposite experience. If there was one piece of advice that I would like all of you to keep with you in class and in competitions it is to actually be aware of the fact that everything you say, every nuance, is noticed by the students /competitors.

The center might be having a conversation with another judge about something unrelated to the competition and utter the phrase "That sucks." The child, hearing just that part of the conversation......you see where this ends.

A miscommunication can occur when the competitor is presenting himself. The center judge, being funny (?) says things like "Didn't your Sensei tell you to wear your WHOLE *gi*?" "Get some patches on that *gi* before you come back." This nonchalant speaking style doesn't take into account that, for the most part, the center judge doesn't really know this student. There are many different types of students going to a competition. All of them have stories of parents with too much money, no money, parents who feed them and dress them before bringing them and parents who drop them at grandma's to handle it.....we don't know each competitor's back story.

Realizing that karate should be character BUILDING, we should not use sarcasm as a means to be funny at the expense of competitors we don't really know. The center judge should keep an eye on the eyes of the competitor and use their own experience and insight to make everyone as comfortable as possible.

Another job of the center is making sure the other judges are quiet, paying attention, and informed of the judging criteria. When the ring ends, and the judges walk over to talk to the competitors, it wouldn't hurt to use the old rule of compliment, critique, and compliment instead of running a litany of why the child didn't win. These simple tricks will make it a great experience for the competitors whether they win or lose.

A Few More Thoughts

Although I love the look on the faces of my kids when they win, I don't stress winning in competition. The main thing that I want children to get out of competition is the ability to take a risk without letting the fear of failure stop them before they have begun. That is a skill that is important in life and lacking in many modern people (in my opinion).

This is what I say to the children before we go to competition:
- *Have fun.*
- *Be a good sport. Learn to win and lose gracefully.*
- *Meet new people.*
- *Do your best.*

We practice sportsmanship in both winning and losing. Although it is MUCH harder to do in real life, it is a fun class and we always exaggerate the bad sportsmanship role – both the winning gloat and the losing pout – for fun and laughter in the dojo. It is an easy and fun way to discuss karate courtesy.

When we return from competition, I don't ask the children what place they took. Whatever they do I am proud of them. What I do ask is: "What do you want to tell me about the competition?" The children all have different takes on the day. Some tell me how they placed. Some tell me who they met. Some talk about the fun, or excitement, or fear. Whatever they say, I accept it, tell them how proud of them I am, and we move on.

My goal with my students is that they look at risk taking as an ordinary part of life. Since the majority of students who enter the dojo are not going to continue to train for many, many years, I use the karate competition to try to create a person who will continue that risk taking ability into the next life experience they attempt.

Teens and Perspective
(August 2011)

The point of today's quick note is that kyus, especially teens, don't always know that they should initiate their future.

Maybe you are a teacher who realizes this and initiates conversations that allow them to constantly progress. Hopefully, I'm not the only teacher whose teens are a bit self-absorbed and distracted by puberty, studies, and games of all sorts.

Years ago, when I realized my teens would be leaving for college without finishing that first baby step of training, i.e. *Shodan*, **I created a dialog with the teen and their parents.**

In the conversation I tell them what the road to *Shodan* **entails. I explain cost and time realities, and give them an opportunity to set up a time-line with what needs to be accomplished.**

This does not guarantee passing a *Shodan* test. What is accomplished is that I put the 'ball in their court' to follow through or drop.

Last quick note: I have had success, failure, and apathy using this method. Before I began doing this, I felt as if I hadn't fulfilled my obligation as the "one who has come before". After all, I know the way and my job is to show students the way. Adults can stay as long as they want, take as long as they need to accomplish their first step. Teens, however, are limited to a short period between 16 and the time they leave for college.

Even if I've been their Sensei since they were 5, there is a small window when they are old enough to accomplish all the details that *Shodan* testing requires and when they are off to become successful at their next challenge.

CHAPTER 5
Seriously! One more thing.

Sensei as an Example
(March 2013)

In the 90's I wrote a series of books called Kicks with Kids. In the first one I wrote: Whether we like it or not, whether we know it or not, our students become what we are, not what we tell them to become. I still stand by that statement. We create strong men and women by example. Because of this phenomenon, I realize that there is a subtle difference between portraying myself as perfect and being an example of a person who is taking responsibility for the very human trait of making mistakes. If it is true that a Sensei is essentially someone who came down this road before the student, the best teacher for any student is one that is a visible example of continuous metamorphosis, change, and growth. When the teacher hides his (or her) imperfections or justifies them, or lives as if the rules do not apply, he (or she) is all but guaranteeing that the student will follow in his (or her) footsteps.

Showing my human side to students doesn't mean letting the class become undisciplined. Here is an example from a recent children's class: I was working with nine students while another Sensei was working with the rest of the class. We were doing bag work. Accidentally, I didn't give one student a turn. He mentioned it courteously and I said "Holy Cow, Sensei made a mistake. Should I do push-ups?"

All the kids said yes, knowing that when Sensei does push-ups – we all do push-ups. We chose to do 10, did them with joy and energy, and moved on. Being human and accepting that I am never going to live a life mistake free is imperative to my personal growth and as an example to students young and old.

A game that I was introduced to as a white belt is called "Sensei Says". It is an excellent tool to work on self-honesty. Basically it is Simon Says with two small changes. We use the word "Sensei" instead of Simon and a person is never "out". When they make a mistake, they do push-ups and go right back to the game.

Sensei Lydia leads a game of Sensei Says to a group of experienced children

The reason I use this game regularly in my kids classes is because I want to teach kids that self-honesty is something that they can achieve. It is quicker than making excuses and more productive than lying to yourself.

Self-honesty is difficult (hence the field of psychiatry). However, it is also imperative to growth. Starting this process with something fun, quick and inclusive of all is a great way to open the door to making this process a part of everyday life.

Sensei Harrison teaches the newer students how the game is played.

One of the most rewarding and selfish aspects of being a full-time Karate teacher is that as the teacher, I grow as much or more than my students with every day of training.

Adding the concept of being myself in front of a class has allowed me to grow in ways that I had not known previously. At the very least, this is worth thinking about.

Glossary

Japanese:

Bo – A staff, or long stick used in karate training.

Bunkai – Term for short choreographed fights.

Chi – Internal strength. Also called Ki, and Prana.

Dojo – Martial Arts training space.

Empi – Elbow

Escrima – A karate weapon that is a stick between 24 and 30 inches long.

Gi – Karate uniform.

Karate – A Japanese Martial Art.

Karateka – A Martial Artist who is presently training.

Kata – Form, a series of choreographed moves taught in a specific order.

Kiai - A loud and powerful yell.

Kumite – The Japanese term for sparring. Go Kumite is hard sparring. Ju Kumite is soft contact sparring.

Kyu – Rank under black belt in a dojo.

Oos (Proper spelling "Osu") – A term that means "Yes, I understand. Let's move on to the next thing.

Sensei – A teacher (In a dojo, the teacher is called "Sensei".)

Shodan – 1st degree black belt.

Shotei – Palm heel strike.

Tekkie 1- The name of a kata (form) in some Japanese styles of karate.

English Terms and Phrases:

Bag Work – This term is exactly what it sounds like; punching bags of all sizes.

Bowing – In karate, bowing symbolizes the karate students desire to try their best to grow and train in the way of karate.

Break – Moves that begin a kata. The moves are defensive signifying the philosophy that karate should be used to defend, not aggress.

Center Judge – In karate competition, the lead (head) judge is called the 'center judge'.

Chamber Hand – While doing kata, if a hand isn't being used, it is kept in "chamber". The exact placing varies depending on the choreography and style.

Confidence Line – As karate training continues a student's confidence grows. This is often spoken of as a 'line' and that line moves, changes, grows.

Fighting Spirit – An internal intensity and focus the student should bring to training. (p.116)

Fire Rope – A game we play in my dojo. Simply put, it is a jump rope game where I tie a long rope to a chair, and while turning it, let the kids jump, or run through the turning rope. The term "fire" was added for fun.

Gaze Control – When, during kata, students look at their opponent with spirit and intensity.

Internal / External Martial Art – An internal training style emphasizes both physical and philosophical strength and balance. An external training style is more like a sport.

Line Up – The words used to start class. When the students hear the words, they make straight lines and stand in Attention, ready to work.

Medicine Ball – A weighted ball that is used for exercise.

Outside Blocks - A karate move that is taught at the beginning level.

Push Ups – In karate, when we make mistakes, we show self-accountability by doing push-ups.

Sensei Says – Same as the game Simon Says only we replace the word Simon with the word Sensei.

Sparring – A part of training where, wearing protective gear, students engage in spontaneous blocking and striking exercises that include physical contact.